# TOWARDS A BUDDHIST SOCIAL PHILOSOPHY

# TOWARDS A BUDDHIST SOCIAL PHILOSOPHY

Amal Kumar Harh

KALPAZ

ISBN: 978-93-5128-079-8

Price : ₹ 485

First Published, 2014

*Published by*

Kalpaz Publications
C-30, Satyawati Nagar,
Delhi-110052
Ph. : 9212142040
E-mail: kalpaz@hotmail.com

*Laser Typesetting* : Gyan Print (AB-II), Delhi
*Printed at* : G. Print Process, Delhi

**Cataloging in Publication Data—DK**
Courtesy: D.K. Agencies (P) Ltd. <docinfo@dkagencies.com>

**Harh, Amal Kumar.**
Towards a Buddhist social philosophy / Amal Kumar Harh.
p. cm.
Includes bibliographical references (p. ) and index.
ISBN 9789351280798

1. Buddhism—Social aspects. 2. Buddhist ethics. I. Title.

DDC 294.337 23

*Dedicated to*

*My Grand Mother*

**May no living creature ever suffer,**
**Commit evil or ever fall ill.**
**May no one be afraid or belittled,**
**Or their minds ever are depressed.**

Śāntideva, *Bodhicaryāvatāra* X, 41
Tr. Stephen Batchelor, LTWA, 1985.

# Contents

## Contents

# Foreword

I am happy to commend Dr. Amal Kumar Harh's monograph on Buddhism in its ethico-social perspectives. As the common run of scholarship goes, writers are found inclined towards treating Buddhism in its meta-physical, salvific and epistemological orientations. There occurs a certain staleness about repeating the worn-out themes of *duhkha*, its cause, cessations, and the way to that. Ordinarily, Buddhist ethics is adumbrated in terms of *Pañcaśīla* and the Eight-fold Path. But the issues of individual and society, duty and responsibility, social justice, etc., are often profaned. The revolutionary elements of the Buddhist point of view *vis-a-vis* the *Brahminical* are not highlighted. Considered in that way Dr. Harh's monograph lets a gust fresh air to blow through its pages. I think its worth publication and speak well of it to its prospective readers.

Dr. Harh has been consistently painstaking in his research, in looking for the sources in *Pali* and Sanskrit texts, and adds his own arguments to make the point in a compelling manner. He has broken new grounds in suggesting the ethico-social perspectives for understanding Buddhism and its social philosophy. His inquiry spans from the age in which the Buddha lived to our own time when Ambedkar burst upon the Brahminical hegemonic complacency. In this respect Dr. Harh's monograph is a short compendium of the ways and stages of the evolution of social thought in India and the Buddhist societies elsewhere.

Buddhist societies are facing changes unprecedented and challenging that call for bold and brave rethinking of the traditional beliefs and ideas in matters ethical and social. Dr. Harh has done a commendable job in pointing out how the modern notion of justice as fairness could be formulated along the Buddhist view of *atman*. There are many such areas where Buddhist ethical and meta-physical view could be harnessed for formulating our present state of affairs. Dr. Harh gives us the conceptual outline along which such attempts could be made.

I am sure Dr. Harh's monograph will surely have a larger perspective for enthusiastic readership, and that will go to add to my pleasure.

**Pabitra Kumar Roy**
Ex-Fellow, IIAS, Shimla.
Ex-Coordinator of Project for Translating
*Mahayana* Sanskrit works.
Central University of Tibetan Studies,
Sarnath, Varanasi.

# Acknowledgements

In undertaking this project, many of my friends and well-wishers have supported right from the beginning. I would be failing in my duty if I do not extend my gratefulness to all of them. If I do not put my gratefulness into adequate expression, I hope, they will graciously condone this lacuna.

It adds to my pleasure to express my special gratitude to Professor Pabitra Kumar Roy, a mentor like figure, who has been a reasonable and constructive critic and serious editor, raising so many pertinent queries for my edification. More importantly, he never got tired of keeping me inspired and that also helped me a lot!

Professor Indrajit Ray, Hon'ble Vice-Chancellor, Cooch Behar Panchanan Barma University, took every care by inspiring me to complete this project and relieving me for one month from my regular teaching and administrative assignments. I am greatly indebted to him and tender him my grateful thanks.

I am also indebted to Professor Raghunath Ghosh, North Bengal University and Dr. Debkumar Mukherjee, Registrar, Cooch Behar Panchanan Barma University, for their stimulating suggestions and constant encouragement while carrying out this project.

My friends and colleagues Professor Kanti Lal Das, North Bengal University, Dr. Pankaj Kumar Debnath, Principal, Cooch Behar College, Dr. Sasanka Gayen, Dept. of Geography, Cooch Behar College and Mr. Brindaban Karmakar, Librarian, North

Bengal University have been supportive both at academic and social front and deserve my humble gratitude.

I thankfully acknowledge the financial support I received from the University Grants Commission (UGC) for framing the draft of this minor research project, and thereafter the quantity of writing this project was completed at the Indian Institute of Advanced Study, Shimla during my stint there as an IUC-Associate. Hence, I am also thankful to the IIAS for providing the conducive atmosphere and space for contemplation and deliberation without which it would not have been possible to write this book. Discussions with National and Fellows/and those from abroad and Associates in the Dining hall as well as elsewhere in the campus have been very fruitful. I thankfully acknowledge my debts to Prof. Purushottama Bilimoria, University of California, Berkeley, Prof. Raffaele Torella, University of Rome "Sapienza", Prof. Vijay Sheshadri, University of Mysore, Prof. Priyambada Sarkar, University of Kolkata and Prof. Kunal Chakraborty from Jawaharlal Nehru University for sharing their valuable insights from varied aspects of academic disciplines, which had often converged, directly and indirectly, on my concerns in the present project.

I must extend my thanks profusely for the constant support and time of my parents-in-law, who have been ever ready to offer any kind of support that I have expected. My wife, Shrimati Nibedita Harh, needs no special mention for the help that she has rendered because she will be sharing praise and blame that comes to me. My son, Koustabh, has helped me in completing this book bearing difficulties with patient love.

Last but not the least, I express my sincere and heartfelt thanks to the Publisher, Kalpaz Publications, Delhi for enduring with the hardships till the publication of this book.

**Amal Kumar Harh**

# 1
# Introduction

Past decades have experienced a proliferation of studies in Buddhism, and the phenomenon is almost world-wide. Thanks to the presence of The Dalai Lama in the global scene, attention is focussed on the schools and lineages of Buddhist thought and practice in Tibet. Tibet holds treasures in Tibetan translation, the entire library of Buddhist thought, the teachings of the Buddha and important works by such masters of Sanskrit or Northern Buddhism as *Nāgārjuna*, Candra Kirti and *Āryadeva* along with the commentaries on their works. In most cases, the original Sanskrit works are lost, only the Tibetan translations continue to exist. Tibetan Buddhism is an heir to what is called the Nalanda tradition. The world of Tibetan Buddhism is the treasury of the achievements of Buddhist thought till the twelfth century, A.D. when the celebrated monastic universities across North India were demolished to the ground by the invading army of Bakhtiar Khilji. With the disappearance of the monastic universities, scholastic activities of Buddhism ceased to show up, leaving its wonderful system of ethics to be absorbed by Hindu thought and ideals.

Whatever it might have been, the Tibetan lineage of Buddhism is divided into two categories. One, the direct teachings of the Buddha, and two, the writings of Indian Buddhist masters on metaphysics, epistemology and logic. These are incorporated under the two collections, *Kānjur* and *Tānjur.* The Tibetan term *kā* means the teachings of the Buddha. Again, the teachings of the Buddha, according to the Tibetan traditions, are collected under the two heads, the *Sūtra* and *Tantra*. The *Tantra* part of the teachings is not available in the *Pali* tradition or southern Buddhism, and it is somewhat unique in being esoteric. The Tibetan tradition holds the teachings as higher in spiritual import and considers it to be meant for advanced practitioners. Buddhism, as it is called, comprise teachings on psychology, neuro-science and the meditational techniques for the control of negative emotions, considerable attention is being paid to these aspects in the researches done in Europe and America. Important as these researches are, one-point becomes pivotal, and that is, how to modulate our negative emotions like anger, hatred and jealously in dealing and living with others? This area of inquiry may be conveniently called a meta-theory from social psychology point of view. At the turn of the new millennium, the Dalai Lama published his *Ancient Wisdom, Modern World, and Ethics for the New Millennium*. This is a tract on secular ethics. In this book, the Dalai Lama has argued that in order to get an idea as to how should one live with others, one need not have any religious presuppositions. Ethics is indifferent to religious beliefs and practice. This is something remarkable, as the book comes from the one, who is the most famous Buddhist in the world today. The head of one of the schools of Tibetan Buddhism which is five centuries old. The Dalai Lama brings us an important message, namely, the primacy of ethics. In a world that is endemic with anger and hatred, the message of compassion and loving-kindness assumes urgency that can hardly be sacrilegious.

It may be noted that Buddhist ethics, however insistent it be on self-culture and self-discipline, essentially recommends a mode of living in a non-solipsistic world. The culture of *brahma-vihāra* is addressed towards the issue of living in a world where there are other sentient beings. The concept of *brahma-vihāra* occurs in the *Sutta Nipāta*, and the idea reigns over both the domains of *Theravāda* and *Mahāyāna* persuasions. The Tibetan philosopher Tsong-kha-pa has written extensively on the virtues of *maitrī*, *karuṇā*, *muditā* and *upekṣā* in his *Lam Rim*. In Buddhism, the negative emotions like, *rāga*, *dveṣa* and *krodha* are likened to poisons, and the meditation practice of *brahma-vihāra* is to be cultivated as antidotes. In this respect, Buddhist ethics is therapeutic in intent. The issue with this ethics is how to regain moral health, immunising from negative emotions.

Śānti Deva, a medieval Buddhist ethicist, composed the classic *Bodhicaryāvatāra* as a basic text of *pāramitā yāna*, the way of perfecting the virtues. *Pāramitā* is a term that stands for perfected virtues, and covers the extensive concept of *Śīla*, beginning with the basic five rising to the ten in numbers. To adopt the phrase from Kant, we may say that in Buddhism, there is no respite from *śīla*. Even the Buddha himself had said that in spite his being enlightened himself, he remains always washed around by *śīlas*. This statement throws the idea of the primacy of ethics into high relief. This brings us to the ideal of *bodhisattva*, an all important term in *Mahāyāna* ethics, even though the term is ancient and found in the texts of *Pali* Buddhism. The Buddha, before his enlightenment, was a *bodhisattva.* The Jātaka tales relate the journey of the *bodhisattva* towards becoming the Buddha.

Bodhisattva is a person who follows deep altruism. He may stand on the verge of enlightenment, and yet postpones entering the state of blissfulness in deference to call to work for ameliorating the suffering of others. It remains a matter of happiness for him to court pains and suffering for the good and happiness of others. This point bears resemblance to what St Paul had said about charity. Charity is what is called 'Christian love'. According to St Paul, there are three pillars of Christianity namely, faith, hope and charity. A Christian has faith in Christ's divine son-ship. He hopes to be redeemed by the grace of God. Then St Paul goes to say that even if one lacks faith, Christianity remains, if one does not hope to be redeemed, even then Christianity abides, but if there is no charity, the out-going love for one's fellowmen, there will be no Christianity whatsoever. Christianity, as per the typology of religions, is a religion of love. Even God himself is the manifestation of true Love. We can refer to John's epistle: "If a man say, I love God and hateth his brother, he is a liar; for he that loveth not his brother whom he hateth seen, how can he love God whom he has not seen" (Chapter 4, No. 20). Scholars like Har Dayal surmises that this aspect of Christianity has had a linkage with the Buddhist ideal of *bodhisattva.* The Buddha once told his disciples: "Brethren, he who would wait on me, let him wait on the sick" *(Mahavagga,* VIII, Section 26, quoted in *The Buddha*, tr. F. L. Woodward, Oxford University Press, London, 1960).

We may inconspicuously assert that Buddhist social philosophy is founded on the ideal of the *bodhisattva*. The morality of altruism is the foundation of the Buddhist path. It is worth recalling in this context that the Buddha had come from a background of tribal republic, which upholds individual freedom, personal integrity, and initiative to betterment of one's lot along with concord in society. There is on record the Buddha's admiration for the republic of the Licchavis. It has been suggested by scholars that the Buddhist thesis of *anattā* or *anātma* is just a meta-physical underpinning to encourage the attitude of greedless and non-harming moral intention. The Buddha had an intimate knowledge of the affairs of the state. During the years of his ministry, he kept commuting between the *mahājanapada,* and kingdoms of Kashi, Koshal, Magadh and Vaishali. He was ever-conversing with the members of the royal households, leaders of society, priests, the common people, men and women from different walks of life. He was both an observer as well as a participant, in the monk's way of course, in the life around him, a paradigm of the middle path as it were. There are *Pali-Suttas* that discuss the duties of the householders, of the wife, of the husband, of the king, and so on. But there is one text that takes political philosophy as a central concern. There we find an caution to the king regarding the obligations of the state and a clear account of the relation between state policies and the welfare of the citizenry. What we find is an admonition to pursue policies informed by a doctrine of the good, which policies are aimed at shaping the lives and livelihoods of the citizenry so as to encourage them towards achieving and realising the good. This text is from *Ratnāvali, written* by Nāgārjuna.

Let us take a quick look at what Nāgārjuna has to say on the matter. We find a clear articulation of a set of basic human values he takes to it to be the responsibility of the state to further. These include prominently an endorsement of the value of learning and education. Nāgārjuna is clearly convinced that public education is an important good, and that the state should underwrite it. There has to be the provision for the welfare of the unfortunate as a good, and as a responsibility of the state, a generous health programme is also endorsed. Nāgārjuna is an economic egalitarian, a proponent of a strong redistributive social-welfare system in which the economic welfare of the poor is a good to be given high priority by the state. He is an advocate of extensive public works that will introduce to the happiness of the citizenry and even of the animals in the realm. To draw the themes as regards the social values to be respected and advanced by the state together: the good society is to be economically egalitarian, the welfare of the least advantaged is the primary responsibility of the state; basic human goods, such as education, shelter, food, health-care, and even a reasonable amount of leisure, are public, not private goods, are to be provided by the state.

Obviously, Nāgārjuna's political philosophy is encouraged by the ideal of enlightenment, and one might feel tempted to compare it with Kant's vision of enlightenment, even though the two are poles apart. Kant's enlightenment is centrally bound up with autonomy, with the supposition of responsibility for one's own thought, conduct and values. There is in Kant an explicit theological conception of the value of autonomy. The autonomous state is valourised in part because it represents the fully developed state of a human being. This strong emphasis on individual autonomy as the telos of human life is utterly foreign to a Buddhist framework. If Buddhism is about anything, it is about Buddha-hood, the end and excellence towards which a Buddhist's life is aimed is the enlightenment of a Buddha. Whereas the Buddhist telos is a conception of the good, however, Kant's is a conception of the right: a conception of a life that is empty of specific values, but specified only in the context of the structural terms. For Kant this enlightenment is specified in terms of liberation not from 'cyclic' existence, but from the authority of ideology and of the organs of the propagation of ideology. Kant argues that the greatest threat to our enlightenment, to our development into our highest and best selves is precisely from those who would instruct us in the best way to live. The content of enlightenment for Kant is not any particular way of life, view or other good, but rather the freedom and willingness to choose some way of life, view or good for oneself.

Nāgārjuna and Kant may have held diametrically contrasting views of the role of the state *vis-à-vis* religion, and of the proper relation between the right and the good. Yet, they share the view that the state is, as John Rawls has put it much later, a cooperative venture for mutual advantage, and that is not a conception without content. Each sees state-craft as aimed at the good of the citizenry, and each sees spiritual good as among the central goods at which the state aims. Kant, however, is silent regarding the content of these goods, eschewing any theory of the good in favour of doctrine of the right; and Kant unlike Nāgārjuna, is a pluralist regarding the good. For Nāgārjuna, the good qualities are for individuals, they are also truly social; they are the good qualities that make society as a healthy one, and not simply its members. Buddhism's greatest contribution to political theory is its specification of a rich theory of social good that can inform a liberal theory of the right. In fact wherever there exist a Buddhist society, the insights of social teachings of the Buddha are interpreted and integrated into the socio-political systems of modern times. In the context of India, the leaders of thought have looked up to the Buddha's message for enlightening social organisation and reformulation of the ideals of life.

This monograph was undertaken to be drafted in the wake of a project of the University Grants Commission, and thereafter the corpus of writing became focussed during my stay at Indian Institute of Advanced Study, Shimla as an IUC-associate, which provided me the necessary impetus from within. I found the study engaging as well as a taxing enterprise. I have not ventured to span the entire domain of Buddhist social thought, but I have engaged only in a selection of themes and issues. Buddhism has a vast literature, both in *Pali* and Sanskrit, and it has had changing phases of thought, and hence it can hardly be brought under a single focus. I have sought to give an account of Buddhist ethics, in its individual and social dimensions. Like all schools of Indian thought, Buddhism negotiates between two master ideas, namely, *saṁsāra* and *nirvāṇa*, and proposes a way of life accordingly. The ethical element has been dominant in the Buddhist mode of thinking, *mārga* and *caryā* have been crucially important in its prescriptions. There has ever been a tension between the meditative and activist ways in grappling with the problems and issues of the human predicament.

I have, on my part, have endeavoured to find out a social philosophy in Buddhist thought based on its ethical principles. I have kept in view the changes that are taking place in Buddhist societies in Asia. It is in society that philosophy comes to life, unless it is lived, philosophy remains something that is hollow, full of sound and fury signifying nothing.

I have concentrated initially on *Pali* sources, though not profaning the richness of *Mahāyāna* insights. The history of Buddhist thought, from *Theravāda* to *Mahāyāna* is a long course of development, and I did not dare to traverse the entire course. I have limited myself with the bare essentials, in a synoptic fashion. But any perceptive reader of this monograph will agree that I have not said anything that is unsubstantiated, but my way of understanding is shaped by space, time and personal orientation.

# 2

# Classical Buddhism in Historical Perspective Roles and Rights: Society and Obligation

There is a tendency amongst the scholars to iron out the difference between the Hindu or Brāhmanical conceptions of ethics and the Buddhist ideas of moral life. Radhakrishnan has remarked that the Buddhist ideas of moral life had been absorbed into the body of Hindu view of life. Tilak considered the issue in his commentary of the *Gītā,* and said that Buddhism rose into rebellion against *Brāhminical* orthodoxy, and founded a dwelling apart after having taken its share of the patrimony. These views are harmless in so far as they go, but belie some hard historical realities. We propose to consider the historical antecedents that led to differentiation the *Śrāmanic* view of life from the *Brāhminical.*

The *Brāhminical* view of ethics is squarely based on the caste-based scheme of society, and flourished under the patronage of monarchs. The middle of the first millennium introduced a new ideological perspective. Buddhism subsumed the new perspective, and it is convenient to juxtapose the polarity of Vedic thought with that of Buddhism. The primary concern of the new attitude is with the perception of change, the recognition that the context during this period was different from any that had existed before. The outcome of this recognition was the growth of ideologies that were at the same time innovative and germinal to the social and religious philosophy and ethical thought of subsequent periods. This carried within it the elements both of pessimism at the passing of the old order and of optimism in having discovered a way to deal with the changed situation. The 'way' as perceived by the Buddha was arrived at through an innovation in ideology, the notion of causation. Causation, in turn, highlighted other aspects of innovating thinking, some entirely new, and others resulting from the extension of existing ideas.

To understand the perception of change at this time and the need for a new ideology the Buddha and Mahāvīra, the authors of these ideas have to be seen in a historical context. The priorities in their questions and the kinds of avenues which they explored in a search for answers were not unconnected with the historical milieu in which they lived. They appeared in response to the essentially urban civilisation of the valley of the Ganga. This was the age of the princes and traders. Tribal identity gradually gave way to territorial identity. The territorial units or *janapadas*, that emerged were named after the *janas* (tribes) settled thereon, such as Kāsī, Kośala, and Magadh, etc. There was predominantly *kṣatriya* oligarchic political organisation in many *janapadas*. In course of time, references to *jana* (tribe) decreased and those to *jāti* (assigned by birth) increased. In Buddhist literature, *jāti* is used in the sense of caste, implying an endogamous kinship group, ranked in a list of specialised occupations and service relationships, reflecting an increase in social stratification. The bi-polarity of purity and pollution remained an important characteristic of the classification by *varṇa*, but this classification was of a more theoretical kind involving initially four, *brāhmana, kṣatriya, vaiśya* and *śūdra,* and subsequently five (the untouchable) groups in society, and eventually became more closely related to ritual than to social status. *Jāti* slowly became the gauge of a more precise assessment of the socio-economic status of a group, but the criteria of status continued to include ritual status or *varṇa*.

During the time of the Buddha a major change in the agrarian structure was the emergence of large estates owned by individual *kṣatriya* families. The criterion of wealth came to be associated more with land and money and less with cattle, which had been the measure of riches in earlier Vedic literature. The slave had the *varṇa* status of a *śūdra*. The intensification of agriculture provided the economic base for the growth of towns in the Ganga valley. Many of the cities, apart from being important commercial centres, were also the capitals of the *janapadas* such as Kausambi, Kāśī, Ayodhya and Rajagriha. These were the nuclei of the affluent and the habitat of *sendhi-gahapatis*, the immensely wealthy traders and financiers. There was the growth of cities that coincide with rapid rise of Jainism, with the prohibition on agricultural professions and restriction on ownership of land. Trade became the predominant occupation of the Jains. The discovery of new routes and the revival of old routes were further incentives to trade. The city produced its own social stratification, where the *Sresthin* (merchant or banker) was the most powerful, and where the institutional base was that of the *śrenī* or guild. This explains why various religious sects competed for the patronage of the *Sresthins*. In the *Brāhminical* literature the trader is not included among the superior social group. Power in *Brāhminical* texts was connected with ownership of land. In the changed scenario land was by no means the primary source of wealth.

The surfacing new society grew into complexity. The *Ārya-dāsa* dichotomy was based on the criteria of using of Sanskrit and the observance of *varṇa* rules. The non-*Āryas* were called *mleccha* or the barbarians or the impure. They were ranked with *śūdras*. But when foreign conquerors like the Indo-Greeks had to be accommodated into society, they were given the status of degenerate *kṣahtriyas*. The formation of new castes had become an open process. New *jāti* arose by incorporating tribes and guilds, and later, religious sects into caste society. The complexity of the new society is reflected in the need for codifying the laws of the various social groups. This was done by the *Brāhmanical dharmaśāstras*. The purpose of the laws is to differentiate between the various social groups based on *jana, jāti* and *varṇa*. The codification did not aim at uniformity of laws, but to the recognition of their diversity.

The Buddhist social code, on the other hand, stressed on broad moral principles of general application to a variety of social groups into new patterns. It was apparent that a condition of permanence was neither feasible nor possible in the world of reality where all were unstable. The conditions of constant change could not be ignored. It affected the assumptions of the philosophers of the time and is still reflected in the prevailing intellectual systems. The consciousness of change is perhaps seen most clearly in the fundamental problem of human salvation or liberation in which the three inter-related aspects were emphasised-namely, the ethic of the individual in terms of his own moral consciousness and his search for release from the bonds of human existence, the verification of ultimate knowledge is essential to the working out of a means to salvation, and finally the discovery of a path to salvation. The prime motivation was to find an answer that would subsume changing material conditions and yet remain viable. The Buddhist attempt to analyse these problems make a point of contrasting the attempts of other groups of thinkers similarly involved.

That these concerns were widespread and apparent from the rise of a variety of heterodox sects, among which Buddhism was included. These sects were not merely a reaction to Vedic religion, since within the Vedic-*Brahman* framework there had also been a diversification of views as evidenced by the texts of the *Upaniṣhads* and the *Āraṇyakas*. These texts show liberation of the speculative consciousness from the burdens of magical sacrifice and ritual. But the author of the discourses sought individual liberation. They preached that through *sannyāsa* or asceticism the individual could find his *moksha* or salvation which would release his *ātmā* (individual soul) and enable it to unite with the *brahma* (all-soul). Asceticism was motivated both by a desire to escape from the insecurity of a changing society and by the conviction that meditation was an effective means of acquiring the knowledge that furthers self-realisation as well as the power (*tapas*) to become superior even to the Gods. Gradually, asceticism came to be regarded as a more powerful force that sacrifice, thus admitting the ineffectiveness of a community attempt to reach moments of magic and power. The freedom insured the renounces a moral status far higher than that of even a sacrificer *Brāhman.*

The Buddhists and Jains had both philosophical and social concerns. Access to knowledge did not lie through the authoritative voice of the Vedas, for what is not personally verifiable is unacceptable. Nor is skepticism a path to knowledge. Even asceticism was not possible as a path to salvation for everyone. Both the Buddha and Mahāvīra, though seeking enlightenment through isolated meditation nevertheless returned to the world of the cities and villages to preach the path of salvation to the householder, who could not become a monk owing to his social obligations. In the case of the Buddha, the emphasis on the middle way, the path devoid of excesses, emphasising moderation and a moral life, was indicative of his concern that the path suggested by him be compatible with the real problems of social existence. Not surprisingly, the supporters of Buddhism were not ascetics but also and in larger numbers, the merchants and members of the *kṣhtriya* class.

The thread of social protest winding through the heterodox teachings was indicative of a perception of change: of existing change, the recognition that further changes were imminent, and towards change itself. For Buddhists, change was symbolised in two strands, which occasionally intertwined, the cosmic and the historical. The universe is transient and in a state of continuous flux. Buddhist cosmic time was cyclical, starting with a pristine utopian society, which had gradually decayed and was slowly reaching its nadir of sorrow and suffering, the direction in which contemporary society, was moving. Eventually, it would rise upwards again and begin a utopian phase. Time was seen as an unending continuity of which historical time was but a fraction. Within this continuity the individual consciousness also moved unceasingly from one life-time to the next birth until liberated from the chain of rebirth. It is compared to the flame of a lamp used to light another lamp and so on, *ad infinitum*. In each case, the flame of the lamp is both the old and the new flame, and so it is with the perception of change in the continuity of time.

Change, therefore, cannot be seen as sudden break. But within historical time there is a far sharper awareness of the past and the future. Other enlightened ones have tread the same path in the past as the Buddha. Was this allegorical, or was it a reference to earlier teachers with a similar doctrine? There is also the reference to the Buddha *Maitreya,* who will reawaken the world to the *Dharma* many centuries after the present Buddha. The decline from utopian beginnings is not accidental. There is a concern with moral decay, which, although partially inherent, is nevertheless caused by changes in the material content of life. It can be circumvented to some extent by the individual's choice in the manner of adapting to changing social situations.

Central to the awareness of change is the law of causality, and it is around this that much of Buddhist doctrine revolves, claiming to derive from rational arguments and examples. At the individual level, the interconnection between desire, suffering and rebirth is explained by causality. The elimination of *duhkha* (suffering) lies in the elimination of *tanhā* (desire), and this can be achieved by observing the precepts of the *Dharma*, the Law as taught by the Buddha and the eight-fold path. Social change is also explained by causality and it becomes a part of the underpinning of the universal applicability of the *Dharma*, for, once the causal connection is known, change comes under control.

This led to a new perspective on the significance of the individual. Buddhism turned the earlier perspective inside out, and the focus shifted to the individual rather than the social group to which he belonged. Up to a point this encouraged a nihilistic trend, as in the case of the Ajivakas. But nihilism was not characteristic of all sects of heterodox teaching. On this question, the central core of the Buddhist *Dharma* is very clear. When renunciation or opting out is not feasible, the individual, whatever his social status, had the choice of becoming a disciple and observing the rules of the middle way. Furthermore, the moral responsibility of the individual was seen in the choice of action made by him through his chain of rebirth. The *Bṛhadāranyaka Upaniṣad* described rebirth as consisting of *saṁsāra*, the trans-migration of souls, to which was added the notion of *karma*, the outcome of the activities of one life affecting the next. The Buddhists modified the notion of *saṁsāra* to exclude the soul and to refer to consciousness as the element that continues, and they appropriated the doctrine of *karma* in its entirety. Thus not only was the individual responsible for the nature and condition of his present and future lives, but the doctrine of *karma* also became a useful means of explaining the origin of social inequality and the creation of caste society (*Majjhima Nikāya*, 1.289. This is made even more explicit in the *Bhāgvad Gītā*, *IV*. 13, composed in the period after the Buddha). Not only was a man's social condition a reference point in social justice, but disease, physical pain and even death were seen as aspects of social justice, although the moral responsibility for this condition rests with the individual

This explains the reason why Buddhism was popular among the entrepreneurs and the life-affirming groups of Indian society: the merchants and the artisans. The life- asserting aspect of *karma* is that, if the rules are observed, the next birth can at least bring better and more prosperous life, if not freedom from the chain of rebirth. There can be, therefore, motivation for observing rules. Moral responsibility was developed into a philosophy of radical change, which would have meant challenging the existing system. The Buddha made a distinction between caste as the frame of the socio-economic structure, which he accepted, and the notion of the relative purity inherent in the upper castes, which he rejected. The emphasis was on an individual's choice of an ethic, but the end result of this had its social implications.

Fundamental to Buddhist teaching was the notion of the interplay of acts of merit (*puṇya*) and demerit (*pāpa,* literally, evil, wickedness), and *puṇya* becomes central to ethical thought from this time onwards. The constituents of merit for the layman are activities motivated by the need to further social good, such as harmonious social relationships and charity, but, above all, sexual control and non-violence. Harmony in social relationships referred not only to those between parents and children, but also between master and slave, and employer and employee in general. This had a clear correlation with the large estates of the *kṣatriya* and the new urban culture. Although the Buddha associates the growth of evil in the world with (among other factors) the institutions of the family and private property (recall Plato in the *Republic*, and Marx and Engels in the *Origin of the Family, Private Property and the State*), both of which, he argues, encouraged sentiments of possessiveness and consequently aggression. He nevertheless projects an undisturbed continuity for both institutions. In spite of its evils, the family did weaken the sense of alienation, and hence there is a stress on respecting kinship ties. Charity was seen not only as a means of alleviating the suffering of the materially poor, but also as the giving of gifts (*dāna*) especially to the *Sangha* (the order of monks). This had the additional advantage of strengthening the monastic organis ation and its relations with the lay community.

It looks considerable persuasive for the Buddha to agree to admit women into the *Sangha.* Family ties were a major obstacle to renunciation, and women were symbolic of these ties. Yet during this time it was only in the Jain and Buddha orders that nuns were permitted, and women were drawn largely from urban society and the royal households.

Non-violence (*ahimsā*), the central focus of Buddhist and Jaina ethics, was less important in other religious sects. Veiled, ambiguous references can be culled from the *Upaniṣad*, but the exposition of the idea as an ethical value was that of Mahāvīra and the Buddha. The Jaina understanding of *ahimsā* appears to be an extreme position involving all created beings and the attempt to preserve them from destruction. The Buddhists tend to stress the ethical question of man's action in furthering or preventing violence.

*Ahimsā* can be viewed in association with many facets of contemporary life. It has been seen as an objection to the sacrifice of animals during the *yajña,* the ceremony essential to the Vedic Brāhmanical tradition. There is repeated mention of the futility of killing animals as a religious ritual (*Anguttara Nikāya*, IV. 42-45). Possibly this coincided with the rapid transformation of pastoral groups into agriculturists, which resulted in a depletion of animal wealth (See D. D. Kosambi, *The Cultural and Civilisation of Ancient India,* London, 1965, p. 105). Cattle provided both labour and fertilizer in agricultural societies, and any depletion was a serious loss. That cattle were singled out for protection is clear from the emphasis in some sections of the Buddhist texts, such as *Majjhima Nikāya*, I. 220. The debate on the inviolability of the cow is referred to *en passant* in the *Śatapatha Brāhmaṇa* (III. 1-2.21), but it is again largely due to Buddhist and Jaina disputation that the prohibition is extended from cattle to violence *per se. Ahimsā* can also be explained as a reaction among the new urban groups to the prestige economy of non-urban societies, who were willfully destroying wealth to no purpose. Sacrifice, it was argued, is essentially an offering: consequently it lies not in the destruction of life but in the embodiment of moral values that become the foundation for ethical behavior: in honouring parents, in honouring all the members of the household from the highest to the lowest, in having patience, meekness, and self-control. The values listed are both conservative and conciliatory. Yet the element of radicalism in this view is the inclusion of slaves and workmen as deserving of honour. At another level *Ahimsā* would have suited those who were discouraging inter-tribal warfare and encouraging the expansion of settled agriculture and trade.

*Ahimsā* also included a discouragement of the use of coercion and violence to justify political authoritarianism, very pertinent to the transformation of the *janapadas* into kingdoms laying political claim to large territories. The suspicion of political authoritarianism may have to do with the fact that the heterodox sects often had their genesis in the relatively more egalitarian tradition of oligarchies and republics such as that of the Sākyas and Vṇjjis. Those most directly affected by war would be the cultivators, whose fields were the prey of marauding armies, and the traders who would be unable to transport their goods, or even worse, whose centres of production would be destroyed in the devastation of a town, so often the symbolic final act of a successful campaign. Possibly *ahimsā* could also underline the ritualised wars that were fought subsequent to the *aśvamedha* sacrifice. Implicit in *ahimsā* at the political level is an objection to even the legitimate use of coercion or *daṇda* by the political authority of the state. The king as the protector should avoid coercion, modeling himself after the ideal universal monarch, the *chakravartin,* who is *adaṇda*, i.e., not having to resort to coercion (See *Digha Nikāya* III. P. 58, Sacred Books of the East Series).

*Ahimsā* might have had an ameliorative influence in situations of tension. Ultimately there was also the ethical and philosophical level. Conscious non-violence (not to be confused with cowardice, a point by Gandhi in our times) was expressive of the highest ethical stand. The credibility of non-violence can only stem from a belief in man's innate virtue. It has been argued that the Buddha's *ahimsā* represented the negative philosophy of pacifism. But the Buddha was not preaching rebellion, rather a conciliatory ethic, as a solution of social ills, the negative aspect of pacifism can be justified. If *ahimsā* arose from an awareness of varying levels of comprehension and reaction, then the point about pacifism cannot be the complete explanation. As a method of social protest, the objection even to ritual sacrifice involving the destruction of life takes on an active and reformative role, as is evident from the continuing debate on this subject up to recent times. It is perhaps also worth remembering that the Brāhmanical insistence on vegetarianism dates to the post-Buddhist period. Jaideva's stanza on the Buddha in the hymn to the ten incarnations of Viṣṇu supports this view. Even Swami Vivekananda held this view.

The significance of renunciation has its own role in Buddhist moral position and relates to the moral and political authority of renouncer. Renunciation is usually viewed as a purely life-denying process. But the renouncer need not necessarily be a recluse living in isolation, he may appear in society and play a significant role. Resuming a function in society after having renounced his ties, one's influence can become both powerful and positive. Moral and political authorities are separated, and the former becomes the censor of the latter. This separation can be crucial to the establishing of an independent intellectual tradition, as was the case in the lifetime of the Buddha. If the renouncer is also in sympathy with the aspirations of a community and if he comes from a background not generally associated with life-denial and renunciation, but rather with political authority and status, such as the *kṣatriyas* of the time, his moral authority is almost unlimited. In such situations he renounces, forsakes one life-style to take on another.

In the Buddhist *Sangha* the adoption of a new name by the monk was symbolic not merely of a new birth in the *Sangha* but also of removal from his caste and status (See *Vinaya Pitaka*, II. 239; *Anguttara Nikāya*, IV. 202). The proximity of all castes within the monasteries ran counter to the Brāhmanical ideal of the segregation of castes in daily living. Commonality among such monks from the lay community broke the food taboos so essential to the *varṇa* system. However, outside the monastery and among lay followers the problem of integrating social groups remained.

Each *jāti* had its own religious observances. Religious differentiations were preserved through the mechanism of caste, as were the observance of rituals pertaining to local cults. But Buddhist shift of emphasis from deities to the abstract notion of *Dharma* was an attempt in part to undermine these religious differentiations. One could say that the absence of a deity in Buddhism inherent in the doctrine strengthened the idea of a universal religion. *Dharma* was the eternal Law, ultimate, timeless, non-temporal, transcendent and immanent. In spite of changing human society the Law remained changeless. It integrated within itself the ethic of the individual, the verification of ultimate knowledge, and the path to salvation. Change was perceived, recognised and understood. But it was not the changed situation that was to be subjected to radical social alteration as much as the law that was applicable in all situations. The law was above the particular and was universally viable. Enlightenment lay in the discovery of this law and identification with it. But the law was not to be kept to oneself in isolation. The enlightened ones must return to the cities and the villages and preach the law. There is the repeated parable of the raft, where he who has discovered the law (the raft) must leave the raft for others to cross the waters on it (See *Majjhima Nikāya*, I. 134-5; *Samyutta Nikāya*, IV. 179-181; *Anguttara Nikāya*, II. 301).

In course of time a sense of mission developed in the *Sangha*. The sense was encouraged by the literate monks, and the monasteries developed into centres of learning. This was a point of opposition to the Vedic Brāhminical approach for which literacy was the preserve of the socially-determined few and which laid greater stress on the oral tradition. As a part of the appeal to the wider audience, the Buddha preached not in Sanskrit but in *ardhamāgdhi*, a *prākṛt* of the middle Ganga plain. At the same time as Brāhminical culture was seeking an *ārya* identity and exclusivity, the Buddha was breaking away from it. The extension of literacy was symbolic of much that the new ideologies stood for, the insufficiency of faith and ritual and the incorporation of reason and moral action in a manner that would have wide applicability to large numbers of people of diverse social origins. The perception of change and the need to come into terms with it were not seen as synonymous with a radical ideology in favour of a total change. The Buddhists were more analytical than earlier thinkers in their views on man and society, but they did not feel it necessary to suggest a complete reorganisation of the social structure. To that degree, Buddhism in its historical role touched the chords of social protest but went no further. The element of social protest in Buddhism was limited to providing the intellectual encouragement and justification for the formation of a new elite.

The Brāhminical and Buddhist traditions arose out of two disparate socio-economic backgrounds, a fact which is reflected in their differing attitudes to human rights. The Brāhmin law-makers tried to maintain the superiority of their own caste. They formulated a system of social hierarchies. Social and often economic and legal priviledges decreased with each descending step in the social hierarchy (*Manu*, IX, 313-22). The Law Books had it that judicial punishments were required to take into consideration the caste of the offender (*Artha Śāstra*, IV. 10). Rights were extended primarily to the priviledged upper classes. The lower orders had only obligations. The burden of society fell most heavily on the shoulders of the *Śūdras* and the untouchables who could claim hardly any priviledges or rights. An important characteristic of caste is that an individual is born into a particular caste and cannot acquire the status of any other caste. This resulted in a check on individual social mobility. Caste discrimination was applied in the field of education. The Law Books are very clear on the point that only the three upper castes were entitled to education (R. K. Mukherjee, *Education in Ancient India*). It was only the Brāhmans and the aristocracy who received formal education. Caste discrimination kept the *Śūdras* away and the nature and content of the formal training kept the non-Brāhmins away. Here the Buddhist tradition was in striking contrast. Not only were Buddhist monasteries open to persons of any caste, but even the syllabuses had a wider range and included disciples of more practical interest.

The Buddhist tradition protested against the institution of caste. It recognised that in the routine working of society there were bound to be social distinctions, but maintained that these should not be exploited to the point of rejecting the concept that all human beings are equal. The Buddha was frequently asked about the relative purity of the four castes and invariably replied that all castes were equally pure. Buddhism was in favour of the equality of all before the law. An offender brought before justice must be judged and punished according to his offence and without any concession to immunities (*Majjhima Nikāya*, II, 128-30; II, 148-54; II, 88).

Arising out of its stern and unwavering ethical code, the Buddhist tradition supported the unqualified supremacy of moral law over politics. Law is for the welfare of all mankind. It saw in brāhmanical law the conditioning of society according to the requirements of powerful elite. The same idea of the application of a moral law and the equality of human beings was extended to all created beings, and this was to result in the concept of *ahimsā*. Everything that has life has a right to live, and to destroy life, no matter what its form, is a crime. The intellectual and moral assumptions of the concept, and its bearings in society, law and politics is undoubtedly a great legacy of the heretical thinkers of the first millennium B.C. in India. The republican background nurtured an individualistic tradition in Buddhism with a strong support for the kind of social and moral attitudes implicit in human rights. Despite the tradition having to contend with a caste society, the rights of the individuals are given due stress.

# 3

# The Framework of Self-perfection

From its beginning Buddhism has been centrally concerned with the moral discipline of life. Ethical language abounds in the discourses of the Buddha. Over and over again we see him portraying the Good Life in these terms: the avoidance of violence, harsh language and all anger; tethering of riotous emotions; reduction of the scale of one's desire; restraint of the sense-life; control of the self by its own inner power; the purification of the mind; the eradication of such evil dispositions as greed and hatred, for example, that lead to evil action; the cultivation of a serene and benevolent mind capable of compassionating all beings without distinction. Not only so, but he presents a systematic methodology of ethical discipline and culture by which one may achieve such virtues. Ethics here is the steady pursuit of a rationally conceived goodness. It is likewise true that metaphysics and religion are largeiy bypassed. The Buddha remained metaphysically agnostic throughout his career, turning rather to humanistic and ethical way of life whose main interest was psychological analysis and ethical culture.

It is also true that Buddhism is reaffirmed in a socio-ethical context in modern India. Ambedkar characterised that Buddhism is morality. He made it almost completely a moral discipline. The ethics of Buddhism may be described, in general, as an ethics of self-development. The nature of the self and its development have two senses. First, as a process of development of the self in terms of its inherent capacities; second as a development *of the self by the self.* In the first sense, ethical progress, towards and including the perfection of the arhat and the Buddha, it is the development of those capacities inherent in human nature of their absolute maximum. Every man is a potential saint; Buddhahood is perfect manhood. And in the second sense, this development comes about only by one's own efforts, the Buddhas are self-perfected Ones. The conception of ethics as consisting essentially of the perfection of the self by the self places the centre of interest, the ultimate goal, and the means of development of the self unto perfection, squarely within the individual.

The analysis of the "self" is of primary importance for any essential understanding of Buddhist ethics.

## (A) ANALYSIS OF THE SELF

### (1) No-self Doctrine

The central Buddhist doctrine about the self is its compounded and temporary nature. The empirically observable human being is composed of five groups of elements called *skandhas*: the corporeality group, the feeling group, perception, mental formation or mental factors and consciousness. The fivefold grouping may be considered in terms of one physical and four mental factors or as one physical aspects, three mental aspects and consciousness per se. The physical is the result of mental states. "Mind is the leader" or formative factor of all existence. "Self" is linguistic convenience pace the famous chariot analogy. The self, improperly so-called is a congeries of functions, formed entirely by the conjecture of elements whose own nature and separate existence are problematic. None of the five *skandhas* can be called self because of its impermanent and uncontrollable character. Of each of these it is possible to say: "This is not mine, this I am not, this is not myself". In a sense, the factors do represent an entity: the individual human being of ordinary experience. The reality of the individual is not discounted at one level, but this is actually of very temporary and illusory sort. There is the Buddhist belief that the emotional attachment to the idea of the reality generates the temporary selfhood. At death individuality of the individual is lost. There is no self or soul of any sort which carries on to another life. Only an impersonal residue or impulse of karmic energy is what is transmitted to a new sentient existence. That energy is neither personally conscious nor identical with the deceased self, one's whole body is non-identical at any two given moments of time. Similar view is with regard to the mental elements. As an individual, "I" is a pattern of physical mental flux whose only existence is in the present moment. The past "I" is not more; the future "I" is not yet. The contemporary and philosophical tendency to deny the separate existence of a self, apart from the content of its own mental status, is confirmed by Buddhism. The so-called "self" is the content of its awareness, no more, no less; as this content changes, so does the "self". There is no self-identical person or soul to be found behind or beyond individual thought and feelings.

But Buddhism acknowledges some sort of continuity, called *bhavanga.* It is that which flows along as an undercurrent forming the condition of being or existence. In one sense the *bhavanga* or subconscious flow of sentience constitutes a kind of continuous selfhood. Conscious selfhood or self as consciousness is not a primordial entity. Without *bhavanga* there would be no consciousness, and the five *skandhas* or self-elements are only characteristics of the mental-physical event called a sentient being. As implicit consciousness, *bhavanga* is a necessary, though not sufficient condition of consciousness. The five *skandhas* may be considered not as entities, not constitutive of an entity together, but as functional aspects of sentient existence.

The basic reason for the assertion of the *anātma* doctrine is the conviction that only as individuals realises the essential unreality or emptiness of the self-concept and experience, primarily with regard to their own personalities, and secondarily, with regard to all other persons and entities, can they free themselves from bondage to the realm of suffering and impermanence. This self-illusion is the root cause of greed and hatred and all their bitter fruitage. We instinctively believe in a self and grasp possessively at other selves and things; we become greedy for more possessions and hate those that oppose us. This is congenital depravity.

Buddhism takes it for granted the changing flexibility of the nature of the self, and the power of the self to change itself. The very changeability of the self means that it is not eternally fixed in one mould, and is alterable in its very essence. The power of the self to change itself is the point about moral hopefulness. As the *Dhammapada* says, the self is lord of the self, and it can give to the self-event a definite direction ethical in nature.

**(2) The Moral Quality of Human Nature**

We have given a brief description of the Buddhist concept of the human self both in its momentary unreality and in its dynamic continuity, and noted that it does have the capacity to direct itself towards goodness or evil. What then is its predominant bias of innate moral tendency? Is the self good, or bad, or neither? Apropos of Buddhist premises, the human situation is one that allows for moral action. It is only on the human level that truly moral action can occur. "Human nature" is rather a name for the opportunity and capacity of genuinely ethical behaviour than a description of any intrinsic qualities or specific moral tendencies. There are some affirmations and negations about human nature in the Buddhist scriptures and tradition. These statements serve as foundational principles for basic attitudes towards man, philosophies of government and education, and legal patterns for regulating human conduct.

There is the basic fact that man is a physically embodied creature, the body and all its senses are viewed as a primary source of many of man's most serious temptations. But there is a way, a type of living, which is beyond the power of all sensibility. The negative or evil side of the human constitution is such that man, as an individualised body-mind being, is temporary and impermanent by nature, yet passionately tied to the world revealed to him by his senses and mind, even though that world is as impermanent as he. Every sense, every physical and mental activity attaches man to his life and environment. This attachment is given the name, *Tanhā* or craving, or lust for existence. This is the deep root from which spring *specific* appetites and desire. It is this lust for existence which produces the illusion of the self-permanency of the self as well as expressing itself in greed for the pleasant and hatred for unpleasant experiences and sensations of this present life. Thus man is a blind mass of ignorant craving. Yet, man is not radically, incurably evil. He is ignorant rather than evil. There are roots of goodness in man as well as roots of evil, which may be awakened to life and strength by the proper methods. Man has it within his power to alter his own nature; he is not fated to pursue evil. And there is an innate capacity in him for overcoming the evils delusion (*moha*). To truly know, in the Buddhist sense, is automatically productive of moral purity. Man needs an enlightenment of the mind rather than a change of heart. Human nature in all its weakness is to be gently illuminated, not rigidly and violently coerced.

What is the nature of the perfection which Buddhist ethics seeks through self-development? To meet the above question, Buddhism proposes a two-level approach to perfection. There is first the road to perfection called *Śīla*, i.e., morality, primarily the external standards of behaviour. These serve as a basic moral code for the individual and his society. Adoption of *Śīla* makes the individual a sober and responsible member of the family and community groups. These basic principles may be inwardised into attitudes and further extended by the more positive ethical qualities such as compassion *(karuṇā)*, loving-kindness (*maitrī*), and sympathetic joy *(muditā)*.

The higher states of mental attainment and self-development are to be based on good ethical character, and final perfection is to be the inward ethical perfection. Explicit ethical analysis in Buddhism is exclusively matters of external behaviour and standards. The higher levels of attainment are implicitly ethical, psychical development. Thus, above *Śīla* stands *samādhi*, the attainment of one-pointedness of mind. And above *samādhi* stands *prajñā* or insight and wisdom as the crown of the perfected life. The perfect One is called the Enlightened One.

The perfected good man, in Buddhism, is the inner-directed person, who makes his own decisions, not on the basis of inflexible principles or dogmatic rules, but from within his own free and intelligent perception of each situation that he confronts. There is some resemblance to what is called Situation Ethics. However, the Buddhist vision of good life is a life of spontaneous goodness. It becomes impossible for the perfected person to kill or take other's property not given to him or to utter falsehood. It may be that between the two levels of moral living, one outward and inward, one based and guided by *Śīla*, while the other founded on *samādhi* and *prajñā*, there is a tension or even a paradox. The perfected person is said to be possessing *equanimity* or *upekṣā*, i.e., emotional and intellectual neutrality. Does the highest life imply a transcendence of the ethical sphere? There is a controversy between scholars about the transcendency thesis. We just mention it, and need not pronounce, any judgment, because it does not concern us in the present context. But this is a basic tension in Buddhist ethics.

What is the type of consciousness achieved at the higher-levels of self-development? In reply, according to Buddhism, it is a non-individualised consciousness. Even the attitudes of loving-kindness (*maitrī*), compassion (*karuṇā)* and sympathetic joy *(muditā*) are progressively extended from those who are nearest and not friendly to us, even to those farthest and most hostile to us, until our compassion (*karuṇā)* and loving-kindness (*maitrī*) include every being without distinction. The mark of perfection is the ability to universalise, generalise, or depersonalise such attitudes, both in quantity and quality; not only are they to include all beings in their scope, but they are experienced with no distinction at all, either intellectual or emotional, between one's own self and other self. The individual self of the perfected person, save as it is embodied in a separate body, knows no difference in feeling between one-self and other-self. Is this a transcendence of the ethical? Is it a kind of super-morality? Scholars do not agree as to the answer to the question.

The Buddhist conception of the self is momentary and atomistic. And it is the no-soul or *anātmā* doctrine, experiential realisation of which is held to be the essence of man's highest attainment. Yet, there is an implicit emphasis upon the active, unitary, enduring characteristics of the self. Here is also a paradox. It is in the higher life of the realisation of the truth of no-self and its detachment that the truly dynamic and unitive quality of the self-appears. Here he realises or achieves liberation from the tormenting sense-world. Here alone it is able to independently and freely chart its own course, completely free from greed, hatred and delusion, save alone the remaining bond of the final physical embodiment. The basic tension within Buddhist ethics may be put as follows: the tension between the positive and negative views of selfhood. The positive may be logically inconsistent, but it provides dynamism within the total Buddhist ethical scheme. How does the self realise its own non-existence, or should we say, the non-existent self? How does it become completely itself? The mystery and the puzzle remains, and calls for practice.

## B. The Self as Subject to Karma and Rebirth: Ethics and Nirvāna

In the previous discussions the Buddhist conception of the self was sketched in a one-life context. But it can be placed in the *karma*-rebirth context, when it is a matter of an infinite succession of lives rather than moments that is involved. The assumption of a series of lives does not change the quality of the self as a series of individualised moments always in flux, without permanent reality or character. This series is simply extended to infinitude in both directions from the present moment. In this perspective the whole concept of development gains vast depth and power. This wider context of self-life becomes important, both religiously and ethically. The *Karma*-rebirth context introduces the doctrine of self with its religious dimension, rather than leaving it as a psychological morality. The notions of *Karma*-rebirth introduce factors of a metaphysical nature and of ultimate destiny into the context of self-development. Buddhism teaches that existence or being at any level is a beginningless series of momentary status. The self is not an entity *per se*, but only a stream of energy whose composition changes at every moment. On the other hand, there is an age-long, irrevocable individuality that can be broken by the power of salvation in *Nirvāṇa*. The passage of the energy is governed by the law of *Karma*. The law of *Karma* is that every action, i.e., mental, verbal or physical, or intention or tangible activity, has its absolutely inevitable result in the ensuing moments or lives of the acting individual. *Karma* is part and parcel of the general pattern of causality present in the world order; it is the intrinsic tendency of each state to pass its essence on to an ensuing state. The law has a moral import. The evil deed brings evil, i.e., painful or unpleasant results, and the good deed brings good and pleasant results to its doer in this life or in another future life. My present character, social situation, economic status etc., are results of the moral quality of "my" past deeds, what are the moral standards by which *Karma* itself is governed, the reply must be that they are those of basic Buddhist morality. One is punished by one's sin rather than for it.

According to *Karma*-rebirth scheme man's estate is both crucially important and a rare priviledge. It is crucially important because only on the human level can one achieve liberation. Again, it is only on the human level of mixed bliss and woe that one can realize that existence is suffering and yet have the capacity to take advantage of this realisation to gain liberation from existence.

Having sketched out the *Karma*-rebirth context in which the human self functions, we may go on to observe some of the specific ethical emphases.

The word "merit" or *puṇya* is one of the most ubiquitous words in Theravada Buddhism. Merit or *puṇya* is the favourable balance in one's *Karmic* account produced by past good deeds. Demerit or *pāpa* is the precise opposite in all cases. *Puṇya* is the totality of one's accumulated or stored-up goodness which will manifest itself in good fortune of various kinds. Essentially one's merit is one's own. Both responsibility for, and fruitage of, merit rest squarely upon each individual in himself and by himself. But in Mahāyāna, there is a doctrine of merit-sharing. There are also suggestions of a collective or group merit and demerit that produce good or bad societies. However, the logical and actual result of merit doctrine is that every action of every sort is rated in terms of its merit-producing power. The total realm of morality, or *Śīla,* is complete with merit-awareness. The standard way of praising the good deed is to call it meritorious.

Merit-sharing is indeed harmony with a fundamental Buddhist hope of achieving higher status of universal goodwill, which is extended by the perfected person to all beings. Mrs. Rhys Davids has interpreted merit as *moral worthiness.* To gain merit means to become more worthy, to gain more and more spiritual capacity which will enable one to achieve sainthood in the end. This is implicit in the merit conception, for that benevolent attitude of the saint, in which loving-kindness and compassion are shared universally and indiscriminately with all beings, is the long-run goal of even smallest generous or loving deed.

What is the ethical influence of the doctrine of merit in the context of *Karma*-rebirth scheme? We can say in this context that the Buddha is the end-result of countless existences of consistent effort towards self-perfection. In those existences he achieved the fullness of moral-spiritual attainment in perfecting the *pāramitās* (virtues): Charity, morality, patient resignation, vigour, meditation and wisdom. Good character is not something easily or suddenly come by. It must be continuously and assiduously cultivated through a multitude of successive life-times. This idea adds an important element to human selfhood. Here is a core of solid character, or hidden roots that may be developed for the future, since *Karma* will guard and preserve them for us and in us. Again, the Buddhist opinion is that human nature tends towards virtue rather than vice. The self is not merely the empirical not-self or our direct observation. There is a larger and hidden self which can contribute to our salvation, if only we exploit its hidden treasures of power and goodness by appropriate disciplines.

Another implication is in respect of our treatment of others. One must not judge them hastily, for they too are possessed of hidden self of *karmic* potential that must be taken account of in all reactions to them. There must be a deep tolerance here because of our knowledge that every man is handicapped by some evil roots in him, shown by his unexpected weakness; and at the same time a great faith that there may well be in him deep roots of goodness that will respond to our loving-kindness.

We may turn to considering the relationship amongst ethical values in Buddhism. *Nirvāṇa* is the highest value, but the question is: Is it the highest ethical value? Undoubtedly, *nirvāṇa* plays the crucial role in Buddhist ethics, it is the one supremely good and ultimate element known to Buddhist experience. *Nirvāṇa* is the unquestioned absolute, and it is the final destination to which all quest of ethical good finally leads. It is that fundamental truth-reality, beside which all else is temporary and illusory, it becomes the supreme arbiter of all moral values at every level in the Buddhist ethical structure.

Everything is judged, in Buddhism, in relation to *nirvāṇa*. Hence let us ask: What is the nature of *nirvāṇa*? Once this is established, we may ask with regard to any action, state of mind, or attitude: Does it partake of the intrinsic nature of *nirvāṇa?* When these questions can be answered in the affirmative, then we can be certain that such actions and attitudes partake of goodness in the absolute sense.

*Nirvāṇa* is essentially indescribable. Indescribability is the mark of ultimacy *per se.* What can be described in words is something on this side of the ultimate the experience itself. Etymologically there is some difference of opinion about the precise root meaning of the term *nirvāṇa.* But all the accepted meanings are negative in quality: the going out of a fire for lack of fuel; to blow out; extinction; cessation. Sometimes it is spoken of as extinction of greed, hatred and delusion or again, it may be termed "freedom from desire" or *tanhā,* referring to the final destruction of all conditioned existence as a sentient being. Sometimes it may be considered as the absolute end of the delusion of the separate reality of selves, one's own in particular, but also all selves in general.

In other sense, *nirvāṇa* is the consummation of the no-self doctrine. Progress towards *nirvāṇa* may be portrayed as the progressive realisation of the emptiness of all selfhood. *Nirvāṇa* is the full end of the self, consciousness in all its forms, as that which makes and clings to distinctions, and hence creates fictitious entities and selves and lays the foundation for future existence, is utterly destroyed. *Nirvāṇa,* in so far as ethics is concerned, is full extinction of defilement, *Kleśa-parinirvāṇa,* the extinction of greed, hatred and delusion, and all other desires that bind one to existence. Given *nirvāṇa,* morality is then no mere pursuit of unrealisable goods nor a merely theoretical structure of ethical ideals. The moral discipline is a strongly motivated pursuit of the supremely Real and Good, whose realisation depends upon the seeing of things as they are. It is positive and dynamic even though the way to it is paved with negations.

Two corollary propositions flow from this quality of *nirvāṇa* as the Real Permanent both of ethical consequence.

(a) Reality is the complete negation of change. *Nirvāṇa* is the great Primordial Simple, that has no parts, no distinctions within it, is eternally the same. This is the only way in which Buddhism knows how to define reality. That which changes is unreal. In the ever-changing Buddhism finds not life and power (as in the West) but death and destruction. That which changes is unreal and impotent. In ethical terms equanimity and serenity, even detachedness are stronger than frenetic activity, because they represent a focus of balanced powers, the possibility of truly realistic and rational action undisturbed by distortive emotions or compulsive necessities. The essential dynamism of all reality is the immutable.

(b) The other implication of the permanent reality of *nirvāṇa* is that it is impersonal. Even though the realisation of *nirvāṇa* in this life is both personal and individual matter in one sense, yet it is the negation of all that is personal and individual. One conditions himself for the higher awareness by the discipline of breaking down the walls of his own separate consciousness and fragmenting the unity of his own mental processes. Emotion and preference are detached from himself and spread to all other beings. His perfection is to become totally unaware of any difference between one-self and other-self in any respect whatsoever. The point is that *nirvāṇa* may be a conceptual nullity, but it is, in fact, experiential fullness and perfection. We may take up the issue of *nirvāṇa* and the scale of ethical values.

Taking *nirvāṇa* as the ultimate good, and goal of all human striving, it should be possible to distinguish two aspects of the ethical meaning of *nirvāṇa* and its effect on ethical values.

(i) There are some values, states of consciousness, and related modes of conduct that can be called intrinsically good, because they themselves partake of the nature of *nirvāṇa*. Naturally such consciousness and conduct characterise the higher ranges of ethical attainment.

(ii) But there are also what we may call instrumental and analogical goods, or those deeds and attitudes that lead to *nirvāṇa*, or are more like *nirvāṇa* than their opposites. Though *nirvāṇa* is utterly incommensurable with anything else whatsoever, it can be said that peaceableness, serenity and loving-kindness in action are more nearly like it, and their practice in attitude and action more likely to lead to it, than quarrelsomeness, agitation and hate. Thus, whilst the instrumental and analogical attitudes and actions are found primarily on the lower level of ordinary ethical-social life, even here we find some genuine likeness to and effect of *nirvāṇa*.

The basic drive in the Buddhist ethico-religious discipline of effort is to rise from the analogical and instrumental goods to the intrinsic goodness of *nirvāṇa* itself. And thus the whole Buddhist technique of religious living is one of effecting this transformation of the lower into the higher state. Thus, it seems meaningful to describe the effect of *nirvāṇa* upon ethical values in terms of this progression. The influence of *nirvāṇa* may be seen as a magnetic attraction of individuals up through the various levels of ethical endeavour and inner realisation until their lives partake of the *nirvāṇa* nature itself.

It should be remembered that Buddhism holds that to concern oneself overly with analytic distinctions is to deceive oneself, substituting a word-game for the actual realisation of what the words refer to. It may be observed also that the progression from the instrumental and analogical to the intrinsic goods is also a progression from the *karmic to the nirvāṇa* realm. It is in the realm of *karma* (or *saṁskāra*) that we face ethical uncertainties and problems. It is here that we need to exercise ethical judgment making distinction between what is right and good, and what is wrong and bad. But on the *nirvāṇic* level this relativity and ethical uncertainty is past. The moral struggle and even the relativistic distinctions are transcended. Only absolutely peace and distinctionless awareness of *nirvāṇa* remain.

*Nirvāṇa* and *karma* and their respective goodness contrast with each other. The tension that characterises their relation becomes evident and reflected in their respective ethics. It may be noted that in Buddhist thinking truth and reality are ultimately one; value and fact are identical on the highest level. This value-factness of *nirvāṇa* has important consequences for Buddhist ethical experience and language. It is held that knowledge and experience must move hand in hand, that each one is function of the other, each is an aspect of a central progression along the Eight-fold Path towards *nirvāṇa.* Unless intellectual apprehension of the truth leads on to a first-hand feeling-knowing awareness, it is indeed not knowledge at all in the true sense. On the ethical side such emotionalised knowledge-in-depth is found to transform the totality of the person's thought, motive and action. Thus, growth in ethical knowledge is growth in character to know the truth is to be the truth in oneself. And also oppositely, unless there is the genuine transformation of the person and the enlargement of his capacity, there can be no true inward understanding and further appropriation of even the intellectual truth. This of course is an existential approach to ethical truth.

This is a subtle shift of emphasis as we turn from the *karmic* level to the *nirvāṇic.* We tend to leave, as though, the inter-personal for the intra-personal good; the realm of historical action with a sense of "agency" for that of mystical realisation. That experience which is to be the guarantee and the incarnation of the verbal truth in actual living practice, becomes an end in itself. An experience of the truth replaces the experience of the untruth.

The movement is reflected in the matter of language, a change in the quality of the language takes place. We move from good persons and good deeds towards the higher realisation of the impermanence of all entities and the truth of no-self. We change from the direct assertive use of such terms as good, bad, right, wrong and evil to "good", "bad", and "right", "wrong", and so forth. We turn away from the virtue of affirmative preference for the ethically good over the ethically evil, to the language of non-preference or detachment, we rise in the scale from loving-kindness, compassion, and sympathetic joy to neutrality or equanimity. We move from the language of personal consciousness of interpersonal relationship to an impersonal relation to all beings-in-general and an awareness of infinitude, from positive terminology to neutral, and in the final analysis, from a fullness of speech to complete silence as best conveying supreme truth.

We may try to understand the Buddhist idea of moral progress by considering the import of the Eightfold Path, its construction as *śīla, samādhi* and *prajñā*. This places the moral elements first. It is the ethical discipline that is perfected first; and it is the meditational discipline which produces *samādhi* and *prajñā.* The ethical logic of all this is obvious. Goodness in terms of inward realisation has a priority over social action. Or to put it another way, as one develops along the way to *nirvāṇa,* he changes his mode of ethico-social action. He radiates moral health and goodwill to the surrounding community, and even to the universe at large. It follows that more attention is paid to the "inner" factors in a situation than the "outer". That is the personal attitudes and qualities of the actors in a social-political situation are more important than stated policies. The most dynamic and effective way to control a social situation is by seeking to control the motivations of the persons involved. The fundamental problem is not the conquest of the physical factors in the human environment, but man's conquest of himself.

The essential nature of the ethical life is the development of the self to a kind of perfection of consciousness. It is also conceived to be an infinitely long pilgrimage through countless existences to a state or condition called *nirvāṇa.* This way to salvation is held to be one unitary path which leads ideally through morality, concentration of mind and attainment of insight. There lies a tension between *nirvāṇa* and *karma*-rebirth, which affects all ethical relations, values and judgments. This dichotomy affects all concrete ethical thought and practice. The *karmic* virtue is the virtue of the good citizen and of the loyal member of the social group to which one belongs. It is that level of living on which the humanistic qualities of love, compassion, mercy, helpfulness, gentleness and the social practices of honesty, truth-telling, sobriety, dependability, etc., are looked upon as unadulteratedly good. Community concern and public service are grafted on to this structure. The *nirvāṇic* goods are not licentious or autonomian, though they do not pretend to conform to conventional usages. We propose to pursue the tension and its resolution in the sequels that follow, and try to outline the historical embodiment of the Buddhist ideal society. All through these points are to be kept in mind: (a) the ubiquity of *nirvāṇa* in all Buddhist thought and practice; (b) the subsumption of ethical values to *nirvāṇa*; (c) the essential discipline of Buddhist life is that which prepares one for *nirvāṇa;* and (d) *Śīla* or morality is the prime foundation of all progress towards enlightment and *nirvāṇa.* And overall, it is the inner discipline that is given emphasis as the essentially Buddhist way. In short, there is a *nirvāṇic* dimension to Buddhist ethics and social philosophy.

# 4

# The Buddhist Idea of the Good Life

## I

### The Buddhist Idea of the Good Life

The Buddhist idea of the good life comprises man's action, his intention in performing the deeds and how he should live with others in a harmonious manner. The interpretation which Buddhism gives to intention may be put us follows: An action is not merely a physical deed, or even volition with a physical result. Action includes in its completeness, thought, word and deed, because each of these activities produce *karmic* results. A "mere" thought is considered to be an action with definite effects. Likewise, an emotion is a deed of sorts. A vocalised thought is a full-scale action. Any action, good and evil, caused, praised, and approved of, is equal in effects or consequences to an action committed by oneself. The full-bodied action of thought, word and deed which is perceptible on the social and historical plane is of more importance than the mere thought itself. The inner and motivational aspect of the deed always precedes and causes actions. This is the first teaching of the *Dhammapada*. In the *karmic* aspect, the effects of a physical deed are more serious in as much as they transcend the present social-personal situation. At the level of *pañca-śīla*, or the ethics of the basic five precepts, intention (or motivation) and attitude are of major importance in judging all actions whatsoever.

In any system of ethics vice always has more legalistic definition than virtue. In this respect Buddhism is no exception. Because of Buddhism's preference for negative statement and its conception of the good life as the controlled and restrained life rather than the self-expressive life, basic Buddhist morality is put in the language of the avoidance of evil deeds and its analysis. Take, for example, the counsel to avoid killing. An act is held to be killing when it fulfills the following five conditions:

(i) It must be a living being (that is destroyed);

(ii) it must be known (by the killer) that it is a living-being;

(iii) there must be a desire or an intention (*cetanā)* to kill that living being;

(iv) an endeavour must be made to kill that living being; and

(v) that living being must be killed through the efforts made (by the would-be killer).

A person who commits an act of killing, fulfilling all the above conditions, may be said to be guilty of killing.

Because of the key role of motivation in all ethical consideration we shall turn to *cetanā,* translated as desire or intention. We take it to mean the motivational aspect of the moral or immoral deed. The Pali Text Society *Dictionary* defines *cetanā* as meaning "state of *ceto* in action, thinking as active thought, purpose, intention, will". Though emphasis is upon the active quality of intention, and the reason or basis of the intension or purpose, this is clearly as near to motive as we can get in these terms. For a man's intention or purpose must certainly include the reason for his attempting or purposing some action, though in Buddhist analysis only the reality of the intention, not its nature, is emphasised.

What it comes to, then, is that Buddhism considers as ethical only those deeds which are volitional. A specific volitional action, while essential to the ethical quality of a deed, is rooted in basic attitudes or dispositions, the deeper character of the actor himself. The most deliberate actions express the underlying moral disposition: this is the soil out of which the act grows, naturally and inevitably. Buddhist ethics is essentially an ethics of intension. Actions themselves are neither good nor bad. *Kuśala* and *akuśala,* literally skill and unskill, are Buddhist expressions for what is morally good and morally bad. These terms are applicable to *karma*-producing volitions and their associated mental phenomena. Qualities belonging to the cause are attributed to the effect. An action is termed immoral when it springs from a mental state dominated by the three unskillful or unwholesome roots of *lobha*, *dveṣa* and *moha,* and moral when it proceeds from mental states characterised by the opposites of those. Here we note the important emphasis upon the central role of intention and mind-state, or character in the Buddhist ethics. For Buddhism, it is the attitude that is good or bad, not any given action. We may take as examples of the worst attitudes, greed, hatred and delusion. These attitudes or dispositions are always bad under all circumstances and in every form. And it follows by implication that the opposite qualities of *maitrī, karuṇā* and *muditā* and *upekṣā* are always morally good. To take the example of ill-will or hatred. Its forms are both widespread and subtle. These are the out-broken forms of malice or even virulent hatred that result in everything from tale-bearing, slander, vituperation and verbal abuse to the doing of physical harm, torture, murder and warfare. But there are also the unspoken, though emotionally felt, currents of ill-will within a person himself, nor are they the less evil or being hidden. As with greed, the subtle forms of hatred are the more dangerous. Hatred in all its forms is sheerly evil. The *Dhammapada* famously says, 'By enmity, enmity never ceases.'

The question arises: Is there such a quality as righteous anger allowed in Buddhism? *Jehad* or holy war? In answer we can say on the practical level of ordinary social relationships the proper moral precepts should be enforced. Buddhism is aware of the necessity for laws providing for the punishment of theft, adultery, rape, perjury, drunkenness, violent assault and murder. The society enforces such laws. Yet in the final ethical analysis all anger of any sort is evil. There is no righteous anger in the Buddha's teaching. Prophetic reformist denunciation would be completely foreign to it. Buddhism is deeply concerned with the process of rooting our absolutely all traces of ill-will or resentment in the individual than with social change. Resentment is to be out-maneuvered by carrying the overflow of goodwill and over to enemies; by reflection on the fact that to wish evils upon another only brings them in the end, by the law of *karma*, upon oneself. Such a discipline is calculated to leave no greater foothold for anger in oneself.

We may now ask whether it is indeed true that motive is the only determinant of the goodness or badness of an action. Mere subjective thinking of an action to be right or wrong does not indeed fully settle the matter. But there is a direct linkage between character and deed. Intentions grow out of character and deeds grow out of intentions as their natural fruitage. When we see a certain kind of action, usually called bad, it implies an evil character behind it. Sometimes the true lineage of a deed is hidden. There are many intermediate stages between character and deed; and some of these are subject to many types of insidious coercion, social and circumstantial, psychic and physical, that limit the actor's freedom and responsibility for his action, so that a deed is not purely and simply the offspring of a man's character. We must finally say with regard to motivation in the Buddhist ethical judgment, that though its inclusion is essential to a true judgment, its identification is not all–sufficient for a full moral verdict.

## II

### Social Ecology and Justice

**Social Ecology**: Our point all through above was to suggest the idea that Buddhist society or social thought looks back to the ancient teachings, and finding their relevance for today.

In the present sequel we propose to bring out some of the relevant points out of the age-old doctrines espoused by the members of a Buddhist society.

To begin with let us begin with the four Noble Truths and the concept of dependent origination. These have deep ecological significance. From the second truth it follows that all empirical phenomena have causal origin. Nothing is self-existing. Everything is caused by a set of causal conditions. Given the causal collocations, the phenomena occur and in the absence of which they cannot take place. The third truth entails that by the removal of causal collocation the effect also gets removed. This implies that no society or social formation is to stay on forever, and changes in social systems can be brought about by varying the causal matrix. And also that both ecological equilibrium and disequilibrium are causal happenings. They are caused by human conduct. A human being is the most evolved species in the cosmic evolution and he has acquired the capacity to preserve nature or harm nature. So all ecological, and social disturbances and disunities whatsoever are our making. We are responsible for whatever system or states of affair we suffer from, and we can change it, if we so will. We carry a universal responsibility not to create ecological or social imbalance and to rectify whatever imbalance or social disharmony we have created because of our folly. All our actions arise from our consciousness. If our consciousness is oriented towards what is good and wholesome, *kuśala citta*, our actions will be ethically proper and conducive to well-being of all concerned. Through our actions we help or harm others and ourselves. All our thoughts, words and deeds are results of our past actions and shape our experiences of the present and the future. What we shall be depends on what we are at present and how we behave in the present. We have therefore to cultivate *samyak dṛisti*, the right attitude towards life and society. At the social and ecological level, the idea of right attitude implies non-exploitation, which means that we have only to cater to our needs and not to feed our greed. We have to avoid the extremes of indulgence and abstinence. In the wake of globalisation and open market economics, we have become selfish, and consumerists and exploitative. We have ceased to value our authentic existence and also the authentic existence of others. Again, ecologically, Nature has its intrinsic value as well as extrinsic value or instrumental worth. We have forgotten the intrinsic value of nature and have taken it as merely of worth instrumental. We forget that we are products of nature and we are sustained by nature. This equally applies to society and social membership. This is the simple principle of interdependence. Buddhist ecology is teleological, whereas the western ecology is utilitarian, materialistic and mechanical.

A Buddhist society, based on the teachings of Buddha will go by both deep and surface ecology. By deep ecology is meant, as per Buddhism, that we have to attend to the functioning of our mind. The very opening lines of the *Dhammapada* emphasise the role of mind in the human process. All good and evil proceed from the mind. Mind occasions our conduct and makes it good or bad. This is the foundation of all ecology and society. This is the real deep ecology that pertains to inner environment, which is crucial for any society.

The surface ecology pertains to our actions that constitute outer environment, societal or natural. We feel affected by our actions. They are visible and tangible. But they are not basic, they result from our thinking, it is there our actions have their roots. Knowledge and conduct are two sides of the same coin, but knowledge is more basic. The Eight-fold Path begins with knowledge. The point is that ecological consciousness, societal or natural, is fundamental to ecological conduct. Consciousness of ourselves and others operates at the deeper level, and actions are its outward expression at the surface level.

There is another dimension of Buddhist thinking on deep ecology. Buddhist thesis of essential unity of all existents implies that the ecology is holistic. It does not go by the nature-culture, body-mind, heredity-environment dichotomies. This approach is non-materialistic and teleological. Hence Buddhist social theory is, properly speaking, eco-ethical at its base, it is a widening of moral sensitivity as it views human actions is an ecological context. Every society needs eco-conduct to solve eco-crises. This is also a premise of engaged Buddhism, irrespective of our religious affiliations. Buddha did not propound any religion of his own but only pointed to a way to eradicate human miseries and sufferings. This is important and relevant for us. The vision of self-sameness of all existences and altruistic longing for eradication of sufferings of others as one's own informs Buddhist social theory, and as such it crosses all barriers of race, creed and countries. This is a significant message for the present day distracted humankind suffering from exhaustion of spirit and languishing in the narrow and rigid confinements of ego-centricism, parochialism and disastrous consumerism.

**Justice**: A good many of Buddhist countries had been colonies of former European powers, and hence the question of justice is of uppermost importance there. There is an awakened consciousness about exploitation and undemocratic rule. Everywhere one notices movements against dehumanising state of affairs being carried on along Buddhist premises. Sri Lanka, Myanmar, Thailand, Cambodia and Korea all are Buddhist countries, and political and social movements, have been alive there by an awakened Buddhist people. A universal precept of fairness and redness, based on the recognition of human equality, is demanded against violations of justice and travesty of universal human rights. Universal compassion, for a Buddhist, is not rooted in any self-regarding element, but rather in the simple awareness that all others are human beings who, just like oneself, aspire to happiness and shun sufferings. The Buddhist idea of unity is human unity, based upon the principle of "interdependence" or "interbeing" as the Dalai Lama or Thich Nhat Hanh has put it.

## III

### Action and Emotion: Individual and Society

For the purposes of constructing the social orientation of ethics three *Sūttas* may be selected for their ethical content. It should be noted at the outset that Buddhism encourages cultivation of social emotions, and such *Sūttas* as the *Mangala Sūtta,* the *Sigālovāda Sūtta* and the *Metta Sūtta* may be considered as the locus classics of our discussion. The Eight-fold Path, the three *Śīlas,* namely, the Right Speech, the Right Action and the Right Livelihood, the Five Precepts and the Four Abiding comprise the moral attitudes for general Buddhist moral legislation. Classical Buddhist texts outline three levels or aspects of ethical living. All these deal with the norms of personal–social actions. The precepts, sometime five or ten in number are the minimal morality, and also basic morality capable of many degrees of fulfilments.

The precepts are largely self-explanatory. But specific meaning and application of a precept in a given situation is possible. When the precepts are five in number, they are called *Pañcaśīla,* and when ten, *Daśaśīla.* Murder, theft, inappropriate sexual conduct, false speech and indulging in intoxicants are directed as *pañcaśīla* towards bodily restraint of the moral agent. The five precepts may also be observed as the principles of non-hatred, non-greed, non-sensuality absolute truthfulness and self-control. The ten consist the Buddhist ethic of virtue. The remaining five of *Daśaśīla* are avoid slander and reviling, avoid avarice and covetousness, avoid enmity and malevolence, avoid self-praise and idle-talk, and avoid wrong, that is, heretical views. They are directed against cognitive and affective non-virtuous dispositions. The practice of the ten virtues prepares one for the proper altruistic activity in society, based upon the meditational volition of the four *brahmavihāras*, sympathetic joy (*muditā*), friendliness (*maitrī*), compassion (*karuṇā*) and indifference to one's joys and sorrows (*upekṣā*). The first three are directed towards others, while the fourth or the last one has one's own mental states as the object. The classical locus of the *brahma-vihāra* idea occurs in the *Maitrīsūtta* of the *Sūtta Nipāta*.

We may begin with stating the Buddhist virtues.

*Dāna-śīla* or generosity with one's worldly goods is the first of all Buddhist virtues. Anything that calls for the sharing of material substance could be classed as an example of *dāna*. Its motivation is twofold: the building up of one's own store of merit and any benefit which it may provide to others. It may be considered negatively as the limitation of the giver's temptations to greed by means of curtailing his resources for self-indulgency, and positively, *dāna* connotes altruism. It also implies public welfare.

Four specific types of attitudes stand out as standard Buddhist virtues. These four are called *maitrī, karuṇā*, *muditā* and *upekṣā,* alternatingly, loving-kindness, compassion, sympathetic joy and equanimity.

The famous *Metta Sūtta* is found in the *Sūtta Nipāta,* and the moving metaphor therein runs as follows:

Just as a mother would protect her only child

At the risk of her own life

Even so let him cultivate a boundless heart

Towards all Beings

Let his thoughts of boundless love

Pervade the whole world,

Above, below and across without obstruction

Without any hatred, without any enmity.

The general concept of *metta* or *maitrī* is very clear. It is a spirit of benevolent harmlessness which is to be universalised. As with similar wish-thoughts, one begins first with himself, then proceeds to the loved, the neutral, the hostile, and finally to the whole universe. In the perfect exercise of *maitrī* one gives to another, indeed to all others, the same quality of loving concern that a mother gives to her only child.

*Maitrī* is higher than sentimental sensual love. It breaks away all barriers which separate beings from one another. *Maitrī* is friendliness and love without a desire to possess but with a desire to help, to sacrifice self-interest for the welfare and well-being of humanity. It is a dynamic suffering of every living being with dynamic, creative thoughts of loving kindness. The basic image is clear. One can radiate a positive influence out into society apart from action.

*Maitrī* is called *bhāvana* as well, it is a meditational practice. According to Buddhism one's first duty is to properly love himself. *maitrī* directed towards the self is held to be no mere self-love, but a benevolent willing of true spiritual character, worth, and salvation to himself. Self-directed *maitrī* aims not at the selfish advantagement of one's own interest and desires, but at the destructions of the ravenously personal elements of selfhood and the eradication of greed and hatred. Only when this is done is he able to radiate to others.

Two kinds of *maitrī,* maitrī to self and maitrī to others, are one and the same and their exercise mutually strengthens each other. *Maitrī*-exercise towards others will purify the self; and *maitrī*-exercise towards the self will strengthen, and inevitably overflow into, maitrī towards others.

There is a pragmatic and experiential side of the *maitrī*-exercise. Only as a man does in truth free himself from self-love, greed, and hatred can he extend *maitrī* to others. The point may be contrasted with the idea of love found in Christianity. Christianity urges men to begin loving others as they begin to live the Christian life. Love of others is a means of livening the lump of selfishness; by deliberate and loving involvement with others the Christian seeks to lessen self-love. He interprets Jesus' commandment to love others as ourselves, as the command to extend to others the same quality of personal concern that one feels for himself. Self-love is not a beginning point but a standard of guidance. Contrarily, the Buddhist does not seem to have any guarantee of freeing one's self from self-concern unless he takes recourse to the thesis of universality of *duhkha* and the metaphysics of no-self doctrine.

But the Buddhist is less afraid of that a man remains stuck on the sandbar of self-love, than that he will try to rush into frantic self-love before he is ready for it. He stresses the unloving nature of much social work–the projection of one's own moral impurities upon others under cover of doing them good; the personal domination expressed in much active "loving" concern; the spiritual coercion of others towards our own values. Learning to love by deliberate involvement of oneself in the life of others is an exception that sometimes works properly, but is not a reliable method of regular operation.

In ultimate goal and even in actual practice the two patterns are perhaps not as far apart as they seem. For the Christian is also aware that the right kind of doing good can only from the right kind of being, or personal quality. And the Buddhist does not actually wait for full self-perfection before he begins to exercise *maitrī* as a means for achieving perfection. Yet a difference does remains. The Christian pattern tends to as the rule towards the active involvement of one person with another in its version of love; and the Buddhist pattern tends towards the detached radiation of *maitrī,* though at present a new activist emphasis and reinterpretation of *maitrī* are observable in such Buddhist societies as in Sri Lanka, Kampuchea, Japan and Korea even to an extent in China.

*Karuṇā* has the general flavour of *New Testament* compassion: pity and helpful sympathy for those in distressful circumstances either material or spiritual. In the Buddhist context it is designated as fellow-feeling for all other suffering beings. It is the pitying sympathy of one, who himself is caught in the round of rebirth-suffering-death (*bhava-chakra*), for others who are likewise prisoners of the same process. And here again the goal is that of spontaneous exercise of compassion that does not or cannot, distinguish between one's own suffering and another, false distinctions between one "self" and another "self" are to be wiped out.

But there is a special Buddhist emphasis which must not be neglected in the interpretation of *karuṇā*. Compassion does not mean emotionalised identification with another's suffering; and the agonised vicarious bearing of the world's sin and suffering in one's own self is quite different from *karuṇā*. To lose oneself in concern for another, says the Buddhist, is mere sentimentality or emotional orgy. It is a manifestation of weakness and not strength.

The ideal compassionator is like a skillful physician rather than a fellow mourner. He fully appreciates the suffering of the patient, but does not give way to emotional sympathy for that patient. Instead, cool-headedly and emotionally self-controlled, he analyses the diseased condition and prescribes for it in a detached impersonal manner. To become emotionally involved would be to undermine his own poise and thereby ultimately to harm the patient more than help him. Only as he himself is calm and pure, perceptive but not emotionally attached can he help another. His compassion must be clear and knowledgeable, not distorted by emotion nor attached by involvement.

This restrained exercise of compassion contains a valuable antidote to that meddling emotionalism which helps no one at all and is so often substituted for intelligent action and attitude. And so far as personal relations on a one-to-one basis are concerned, it is quite true that emotional disturbance in another is more often healed by emotional poise and calm in the healer than by counter-disturbance. Whether it furnishes a dynamic or adequate social motivation is perhaps quite another matter.

*Muditā* has a special quality of its own whose successful exercise indicates great ethical maturity. It is the capacity for sympathetic joy in another's joy or success, forgetful of one's own success or failure, distress or happiness, and totally without any envious or jealous feeling. It is the analogue on the happy side, to compassion on the unhappy side of human life.

Sympathetic joy is undoubtedly a difficult attainment except on those rare occasions in which another's good fortune is our own, either in physical fact or by social linkage. Ordinarily the good fortune of another does not include us. As often as not the good fortune of another only reminds us of our own failure or misfortune. Or even more poignantly, in the usually competitive situations of life, another's good fortune is actually our misfortune, for both of us have been striving for the same prize, but only one of us can gain it. The perfection of *muditā* in this situation would be a real joy, indeed a completely joyful participation in the other's success as though it were our own. Must one wait until he has become a saint or *arhat*, who no longer competes with anyone for anything and whose consciousness has been purified of any distinction between own-self and other-self, before he can exercise *muditā*? Again, the answer is, No! One may and might to begin doing so even now, or whatever level of attainment he may be. For the *arhat*'s perfection is built only out of countless previous and imperfect efforts to exercise *muditā* under all circumstances.

*Upekṣā* or equanimity represents the upper limit of morality. With the higher development or universalisation of *maitrī-karuṇā-muditā* one can see the trend towards the nirvanisation of the ethical. With *upekṣā*, the crown and fruition, one moves into the realm of the ethics of *nirvāṇa*. We may call it the ethics of equanimity.

There is a *nirvāṇic* quality of life. To give it specific form in the nature of a given code of action, precise definitions of what is right and wrong, or even what attitudes one "should" have, is most difficult. *Nirvāṇa* as the ineffably transcendent ultimate value exercises a most potent influence in the Buddhist ethical structure, but likewise an influence almost ineffable in nature. Shall we say that it is the power of ethical dislocation?

The other three, *maitrī, karuṇā* and *muditā* may not be thought as leading up to the fourth, *upekṣā* like stair steps, each one of which is left behind in turn. They work together as a team, each strengthening and complementing the other. Yet, equanimity is nearer to *nirvāṇa* in quality than such activist attitudes as loving kindness and compassion. We may also say that as *maitrī, karuṇā* and *muditā* are generalised in their expression they become more and more like *upekṣā*.

*Upekṣā* has been variously translated as "indifference", "neutrality" and "equanimity". Buddhist scholars prefer the last one. Whatever term we adopt, something of its quality is evident: controlled balance of mind, emotional non-attachment or neutrality, and beyondness with regard to ethical uncertainties and struggles. It is seemingly a calm detachment. Societies may come and societies may go, political ideologies rise and fall in favour, cultures appear, flower and pass away, but equanimity and the quest for *nirvāṇa* go on forever. The possessor of equanimity goes on, unshaken emotionally or mentally by the world's mental, moral or social disturbances.

We have observed that in Buddhism the quest of the ultimately good inclines towards inward states of realisation and away from outward action. If this is what defines the perfect deeds, one may ask if a creation of *nirvāṇa* the same as the "good" deed, which is the product of *karma*. Is *nirvāṇa* caused? In Buddhist terminology, *nirvāṇa* is said to be *asanskṛta dharma*, which is "uncaused".

*Karmic* goodness belongs to the category of ordinary virtue, practising *dāna śīla,* fulfilling one's obligations to society, cherishing *maitrī, karuṇā, muditā* etc. But the perfect deed is so far different. It is the product of equanimity rather than compassion, and it rises above merely ethical goodness. It belongs to the realm of emotional immutability, without any feeling of pity, concern or distress or earthly condition. Of course, there are other opinions about the matter.

But, in the mean time, we may continue with our argument. A deed is perfect because there is no emotional attachment of any sort involved in it, one does it in the spirit of complete disinterest. And since there is no emotional clinging to the deed or its results, no *karmic* consequence, either good or bad, results. Hence the perfection of the perfect deed is not outward, objective in nature, but the inward attitude of its doer. It is the inward attitude of detachment that makes the difference between a good deed and a perfect (*samyak*) deed.

The meditational discipline is incorporated in the Eightfold Path. Its indispensable basis is *Śīla* or morality. Then comes the stage of meditation to achieve *Samādhi.* But this does not amount to salvation. The *vipasaṇā* meditation's goal is the attainment of *prajñā* and *its* perfection results in *nirvāṇa.*

*Nirvāṇa* conquers *karma* and its entire works, good and bad. What must be done is done and the perfection the deed is that the *arhat* who is totally free from his past, because it has meditationally burned up. By the same process he has been purified completely in his inner motivation from all greed, hatred, delusion, and desire to come to rebirth (*tanhā*! *bhava)*. Such is the ultimate fruition of the ethics of equanimity

There are two types of ethical valuation and practice found in Buddhism, that of *karma-rebirth* realm and that of *nirvāṇa.* They are not the same. For the polar attraction of *nirvāṇa,* the Supreme Good, exerts a disturbing force throughout the *karmic* ethical structure. What is good in terms of the ethics of equanimity is largely unknown to the moral striver in the realm of *karma*. Even the prospect of *nirvāṇa* disturbs his sense of right and wrong.

The Rebirth ethics works through *Śīla* in the doing of conventional good deeds and the cultivation of the moral dispositions proper to life at that level. It seeks to produce that solid body of virtuous habits and dispositions in the individuals which are usually termed character. This it does by means of making ethical distinctions between goodness and evil on the *karmic* level. On the other hand, the technique of the ethics of equanimity is meditational. Here attention is turned to the internal aspect of deeds. The technique is calculated to produce a certain state of consciousness within the individual, not a given set of actions. Its chief virtue is detached serenity, or through detachment from that very world of active dispositions and citizenly deeds in which *Śīla* operates. Though the ultimate goal of both ethics is reputedly the same, their respective routes to it are radically different. The logical goal of any rebirth is better rebirth, one that is more pleasant or at least no worse than one's present situation. This is *Karmic* success, and it spells *nirvāṇic* failure.

*Nirvāṇa* as a goal is quite the other. The way it leads in what seems to be a sheerly opposite direction. The road to *nirvāṇa* takes off on a tangent into a totally different dimension. Theravāda and Mahāyāna interpretations differ on this issue, but it is hard to conclude that the two ways, of *Karma* and *Nirvāṇa,* are one and the same way. Within Buddhism, of course, it is insisted that they are identical.

We may elaborate the issue a little further to render it perspicuous. The essence of rebirth ethics is good deeds done in the world of time and space with a view to achieving a better personal status in that same world in the future. It is an active involvement in the concerns of right or wrong in each separate life and in each age. But the ethics of *Nirvāṇa* is completely different. It is the turning of the self in upon itself, the achievement of blessed states of consciousness that are good and satisfying in themselves. The former is consequentialism, while the latter is deontological.

*Nirvāṇa* ethics requires withdrawal from the active life of historical involvement into a life of intense contemplation. It is the search for an experience of the timeless and ultimate, and it is utter detachment from good and evil, right and wrong, and from the distinctions of the intellect itself (*avitarka*).

It may be observed further that the description of two entirely different modes of life have come to be embodied in the way of the layman and of the monk. The way of Rebirth ethics is the layman's way. He can scarcely hope for *Nirvāṇa* and has not the appetite for it in any case. The *nirvāṇic* ethics is enshrined in the way of the monk, who, giving up all domestic, social, economic and political concerns, turns to seek the greatest of all goods. The *Sangha* is the institutionalisation of the ethics of *Nirvāṇa.*

The antithesis of the two ethics has been qualified and moderated in Buddhist societies throughout history, but the logical difference between them remains. It is yet possible to argue that theoretical contradictions intrinsic to doctrinal structure often serve as creatively related poles producing a dynamic situation by virtue of their theoretical opposition. The point and situation is, however, not exclusive to Buddhism, it can be observed equally in Hindu and Jaina societies. For the Hindu, the *puruṣārtha* of *mokṣa* hardly goes logically along with others like, *dharma, artha*, and *kāma*. Transition from the lower ones to the highest is not logically entailed. Again, the *Śramanic* tradition of Jainism the state of *kaivalya* is hardly entailed by the *anubratas* etc.

In the situation, in order to come out of the impasse, we may think of some other mode of understanding. We may suggest that the two ethics are complementary to each other. Moral decency and discipline are absolutely indispensable precondition (i.e., necessary) of the practice of the higher virtues of *samādhi* and *prajñā*. No one leaves *Śīla* behind him as he climbs the ladder towards *Nirvāṇa,* it must go with him in practice and attitude, all the way there. It only becomes more inwardised, being transformed from the mere keeping of perceptual morality in outward action into the attainment of complete purity of motive and emotion and the eradication of greed and hatred. We can think of the cross-fertilisation of *karmic* and *nirvāṇic* ethics, or values. It is possible to have or work out a harmony of values.

Equanimity or *upekṣā* is then not mere neutrality; it works hand-in-glove with *maitrī, karuṇā* and *muditā.* Love imparts to equanimity its selflessness, its boundless nature, compassion, greeds, equanimity from falling into cold indifference, and keeps it from indolent or selfish isolation. Sympathetic joy gives equanimity the mild serenity that softens its stern appearance. It is the smile on the face of the Enlightened one.

# 5

# A Buddhist Social Theory: The New Situation and Response

There has been the tendency in Buddhism towards *karmanization* of *nirvāṇic* values, and the smoothing over of the contrasts between the two value-realms in favour of the layman. This has many roots, historically and doctrinally, which cannot be discussed here. But that it has occurred seems clear. The contemporary world, political and cultural climate is pushing Buddhist cultures towards the *karma* pole. They are being subjected to the pressures of scientific technique and economic expansion. Thus, do Buddhists become more and more aware of the demands of this space-time world, and concerned to build a good society on this earth?

There is also a strong new emphasis on the availability of *nirvāṇic* peace, on a more direct meditational technique for achieving equanimity and inner peace, which has nothing to do with technological progress at all. This only shows that *Nirvāṇa* and its ethics also have value for this present world, and may even facilitate towards the optimum of happy living here and now in space-time.

Thus have *Karma* and *Nirvāṇa* joined forces for the good of the world? Love, compassion and sympathetic joy continue to emanate from the mind and act upon the world, but being guarded by equanimity, then cling nowhere, and unweakened and unsullied they return to the saint who radiates them. How central is it to the Buddhist concern to build a good society in time and space? What would be the ideal Buddhist society, and the role of layman and monk within it? What should Buddhism do to counteract the urgent materialism and the desire for political power in Asia today? Can a combination of equanimity with love, compassion and sympathetic joy, radiated with full benevolence to all beings, meet the needs of the day? These are pressing questions that face Buddhist ethics today.

Yet, Buddhism has indeed created a social pattern according to its own convictions of goodness and rightness; and in this pattern there is a certain social philosophy. This philosophy Buddhism is now seeking to articulate, implement and relate to the present situation. To the consideration of that philosophy and its implementation we shall now turn in what follows:

From the West have come the two most explosive and dynamic forces to be found in the contemporary world; nationalism and Marxism. In a word, the Western mind is socially, politically, and historically conscious in its every fibre, ever since the days of Plato. Compared to that can one find a social theory in the East and in Buddhism in particular? In reply, we may begin by noting that the general cultural context out of which Buddhism developed was religio-philosophical rather than socio-political in its genius and outlook. And though Buddhism had important social repercussions, it was not basically or consciously a social reform movement aiming at the production of a certain type of society. Buddhism is largely a historical in viewpoint. It deals not with man in society or among his fellows, but with the individual man facing his eternal destiny. And it turns man supremely towards seeking a good (*nirvāṇa*) above all space and time orders.

To tell the truth, the Buddhist had little, either of concern for society as such or of firm conviction of its possible improvability. To be sure, there was an existing society and it was not to be destroyed. And there would always be a society as long as there were human beings in some sort of universe. But its fluctuations, the rise and fall of its empires and social orders, its improvement and decay, its forms and names, represented for the Buddha only the stage on which each man plays his solitary drama. Social conditions might help or hinder that man in his progress towards *Nirvāṇa* to some extent, but they could never be fundamentally bettered. Serial orders would revolve perpetually within the conditioned *Karma – Nirvāṇa* cycles, but arrive nowhere in particular. No real *salvation* was to be found in the socio-historical context or in the improvement of its forms. This means Buddhism on the whole has surveyed political forms with supreme indifference. And again, Buddhism took the monarchical form of secular government and society that it found in India for granted and was not concerned enough to worry about changing it.

The *Mahāhamsa Jātaka* tells us that a king should have true counsellers, avoid oppression, punish the bad and reward the good. The kingly virtues should be: almsgiving, justice, penitence, meekness, mildness, peaceableness, mercy, patience, charity, and moral purity. The *Sona–Nanda Jātaka* records the four duties of the king as follows: giving of gifts, affability, beneficient rule, and impartiality. The portrayal of the good king in the *Sumangala Jātaka* is also significant in this regard.

The idea of the Universal Monarch was taken over by Buddhism from its earlier sources. With this background and history little analytic thought was given to political or social matters in Theravāda countries. Now this brings us near to a fundamental Buddhist doctrine, which serves as the *basic social axiom* of Buddhism, and may be stated as follows:

The individual progress is, after all, the social progress. In other words the goodness of society is but the sum of the goodness of its component individuals. Good personal character will result in good community character; which will in turn result in good national character; which will in turn produce good international relations. If every individual gains peace within his own heart, then world-peace will come. Ergo, the method of working for world-peace is primarily to cleanse one's own heart of greed, hatred, and delusion. And since these latter are nourished by the illusion of the reality of the self, one should begin to work for world-peace by purifying himself of the error of self-illusion through meditation.

Reinhold Niebuhr, in his *Moral Man and Immoral Society*, has raised the following questions: Does personal virtue carry directly over into social virtue? And are the two actually the same in fact? Does individual "progress" mean the same as social "progress"? Let us see how Buddhism faces these questions.

There has been such talk about "practical Buddhism", and it means that the Buddha evokes in man the determination and desire to strive in leading such a life as will make for economic, social, intellectual, moral and spiritual progress. We may ask, what is that energy and determination in the Buddha's teaching that produces economic development, social reform, and political democracy? Does the man going on to the perfection of *Nirvāṇa* automatically become a good citizen?

Given such a basic philosophy of social progress, how does Buddhism propose to achieve that progress? Or social intentions? Though there has been a minimum of overt social philosophy in Buddhism it has not been completely without a socially formative dynamism and sense of direction. Such sense of social direction as Buddhism has had grows directly out of one of its basic notions. It may be put as follows: The "method" of social change proper to Buddhism is that of the individualised radiation of virtue out into society by ethically perfected persons. Virtue here of course refers not to specific character traits so much as moral worth, mental–moral integrity or good character. For just as social improvement is held to be the sum of the individual self-improvement of the members of a society, so the Buddhist view is that society must, or may, improve by individuals in a strictly individual way–by the radiation of their personal virtue or holiness. This general point, of course, is common to many moral and religious philosophies: The power of the example of a good man is great and may do more to change the character of a society than all manner of political schemes and policy statements, witness Gandhi's influence on Indian politics and society in the three decades before Indian independence. There is a kind of contagion of goodwill. We can ask: How can good policies be carried out by morally evil men? For, the character of a man affects all that he does. There are no impersonal deeds.

We may call it the ideal Buddhist method of social change, not the mechanics of laws, reform programmes, and political maneuvers, but the reform of the inward character of members of the community spreading out from a central source of holiness. Thereby a given society may be healed of its divisions, strifes, illness, and find wisdom and strength to solve its problems.

Let us note the manner of the actual historical progress of Buddhism through the countries of Asia and its "method" of influencing the societies and cultures into which it came. Buddhism never had a "reform programme", or that it had a blueprint of the Buddhist social ideal applied to a given social situation after the manner of Marxism or in terms of Five–Year Plan. Its approach to a society can be called rather penetrative and infiltrative. It seeks to convert individuals to its faith. Buddhism values and needs state support like all other religions. A converted monarch may swing the whole nation Buddha–ward. This has had happened in Tibet, Mongolia, Sri Lanka, Myanmar. But usually Buddhism has not sought to impose reforms upon the populace from above and to make men good by law. However, passively Buddhism has entered the cultures that have come to be Buddhist in some sense or other, it has importantly modified them. Art and literature have been transformed into the Buddhist image as thoroughly as Christianity modified European culture up to the medieval period. A gentling effect upon Buddhist cultures in general and especially with regard to the taking of human and animal life.

We may now define or describe the central and guiding image of Buddhism in its process of social change. In conformity with the penetrative and permeative method of social change, the Buddhist method grows out of the basic conception of the power of individually radiated moral virtue. The result is what we may call an image of the Good Buddhist Society, towards which Buddhist thought and practice gravitate and which has been approximated in many actual Buddhist cultures. The Good Society is a society in which the Buddhist morally perfected person living in the midst of a holy community radiates virtue and social health into the surrounding society of lay believers. The social value of the morally perfected persons is to be found in their spiritual attainment. Here is a kind of holiness in depth at the centre of society.

As for a secular variety of Buddhist social philosophy one will have look back to the Mauryan King Aśoka. In his case we have an application of Buddhist political philosophy and method to an actual situation on a large scale. In two of his Edicts he sets forth his philosophy of ethical goodness: there is no better work than the welfare of all the people. In another Edict he defines the essence of dharma as "little sin, many good deeds, mercifulness, charity, truthfulness and purity." Perusing Amulyacharan Sen's summary of Aśoka's Edicts, no one can attempt to distract from the height and nobility of his social ideals. What government anywhere in the world, before or since, has done better in this respect? Here is a large-spirited, far-sighted, humanitarian statesmanship of the first order. Aśoka did not regard his pattern of government as being specifically Buddhistic, but within the bounds of the general Indian pattern of social morality. Sen notes that typically Buddhist doctrines like *Nirvāṇa,* universal sorrow, impermanency of no-soul, and the chain of causation, etc., are never mentioned by Aśoka. And K.M. Panikkar, in his *Survey of Indian History* remarks that the secular role of the king is noticeable in Aśoka, he called himself the beloved of the gods, *devanām priya,* when Buddhism has no gods, and he remained entirely in the layman's sphere of values and actions. His practical morality is almost indistinguishable from that of contemporary Indian varieties.

Now the question is: what role does the *Sangha* play in delineating the Buddhist social ideal? In reply it can be said that the *Sangha*, as holding up to the Buddhist ideals is a non-coercive, non-authoritarian, democratic society where leadership comes only from good moral character and spiritual insight (recalls the role of the guardians in Plato's *Republic*). In the *Sangha,* everyone confesses his sins to his brother, where all goods are held in common possession and everyone, high and low, eats and dresses alike. It is an order of society which has no political ambitions within the nation, and in whose ranks there is no striving for leadership. It is dedicated to the attainment of salvation for oneself, the nourishment of fellowship and brotherhood with one's fellow-seeker, and the welfare of all beings. It seeks to persuade men to follow its way, by example and exhortation, but does not attempt to force any man into faith. The Buddhist *Sangha* is a gentle democracy of the spiritual quest for life's ultimate good, and thus it manifests convincingly the Buddhist ideal of the Good Society. Here is the practice of the ethics of equanimity in actual historical existence.

Altruism is built into the programmatic existence of the *Sangha.* The Buddha admonished his disciples to go forth for the good, happiness and welfare of the people: *vahujana sukhāya*, *vahujana hitāya*. The members of the *Sangha* are under the obligation to teach the laity, to provide medicine to the sick, impart educational instruction. The *Sangha* is an institutionalised order and it takes up the task of education as such, that is, education of the young.

The *Sigālovāda Sūtta* is usually referred to as dealing with the norms of the conduct of the ordinary Buddhists. The *Sūtta* divides human relationships into six basic types and prescribes their respective duties. The *Mangala Sūtta* covers much the same ground though in a more general way. So far as the social situation itself concerned, there is no prescription for a good society or the ideal structuring of human relationships. There is no possible doctrine of social revolution or change of any sort. All that is called for is that each man does his duty with faithfulness and gentleness in the place or relationship where his destiny has put him. The values that are mentioned here are the purely individualistic ones of personal attitude and habit. There is indeed little that is characteristically or peculiarly Buddhist in these prescriptions. The question is: can a total social philosophy be erected on such meagre material? In reply it can be said that Buddhism today under compulsion of new conditions is most eagerly seeking to socially orient the basic Buddhist way of life and to find a warrent for such orientation in the scriptures. It is representative of a new and important trend in Buddhism towards a social philosophy.

Such is the portrait of the traditional basis for the Buddhist social ethics in terms of its central imagery, its scriptural pronouncements, and some historical instances of its implementation. The questions that now confront us are these two: What is it that we actually have as a basis in the tradition? (This may be asked in case of Hinduism as well). And how can this tradition be adopted to modern conditions?

There is in the Buddhist tradition the basic imagery of the morally perfected person within a holy community that permeates the society about it. To a considerable degree Buddhist societies have conformed to this pattern. But this is an ethics of transcendent personalism, radiation of spiritual strength and moral vitality, rather than specific social techniques or practical plans. This is essentially the ethics of the monk that may stimulate the layman to be better, more confident, and more resourceful. It is this aspect of Buddhism that is being rejuvenated in new emphasis: the *nirvāṇic* absolutes are being brought into touch with the *karmic* and practical realm, and a living synthesis is being attempted between the two in the person and the practice of the new man in Buddhism. What will be its results? Will the cross-fertilisation of the two streams: monk's discipline and the householders' life really succeed? And what will be the resources within the Buddhist tradition for such a synthesis? This latter question is, of course, one which Buddhism is today asking itself. It is diligently searching the tradition for new answers for new situations.

A tradition actually is what one finds within it. And one of the most fascinating aspects of the contemporary ethical situation in Buddhism is what is being found in ancient tradition to fit the current need. These are attempts to fill old words with new meanings, to reinterpret the Buddhist tradition in contemporary terms, and some of the efforts to deliberately create a Buddhist social philosophy.

Our portrayal of Buddhist social morality has been that of a morality of personal relationships rather than a social philosophy. Its basic approach to any social situation that needs change is the simple statement that society can be made perfect by perfecting the individuals who compose that society. Such personal goodness in the leaders of the world, as well as in their followers, will solve all the complicated problems of economics and politics, and peace with the individual will bring peace to the nations. There is a tension that produces an ambiguity in the actual social response which Buddhism makes to contemporary situation.

We may, following sociologists, speak of "high" Buddhism *of the path to Nirvāṇa*, embodied in the monastic way of life, and the "low" Buddhism of the ordinary layman who aspires at most to the material rewards attending the accumulation of good *karma*. The questions can be asked: which is to be the morality of Buddhism?

Does Buddhism have one, or two, moralities? These questions are particularly crucial as Buddhism faces the new day which is now dawning in Buddhist culture. The traditional pattern of Buddhism in Theravāda nations of Southeast Asia was one fitted to the simple agrarian society of small social units. Now changes are coming up in the forms of military rule, communism, demands for secular democracy and nationalism. How is Buddhism to meet them? In Buddhist countries the *Sangha* had shared power in the past. The prevailing view-point is that organised religion and politics should be kept apart. Politics and religion had come to be at loggerheads when China invaded Buddhist Tibet. In India, the Buddhists are a minority, though there is assertion on the part of the socially depressed classes against socially discriminatory practices by converting to Buddhism. The new generations of Buddhists are emerging as a political force. This may be described as activating and socialising the Buddhist tradition. In this we see the depth to which contemporary Buddhism is being stirred by new situations arising out of demands of democracy and the presence of Marxism as a political alternative.

What then shall Buddhism do with its doctrine of *karma* which seems to bind each man irrevocably to his present social status and personal circumstances? Ambedkar has denied that *karma* is a doctrine of despair. In Buddhism, it may be noted, there are three types of *karma,* in terms of temporal sequence. There is *past karma* which cannot be altered or evaded, and it may be "burned up" by *Vipāsanā* meditation. Thus, the major aspects of one's present life are largely determined. *Karma* as a principle of explanation of present inequalities is thus always *past karma,* and past *karma* only. This has been its traditional use for the most part for those humble people who had little hope of changing their lot in a static society. This was passive in connotation.

But there are two other varieties of *karma*: present and future. Future *karma* does not exist in actuality, though its seeds may have been shown in the past. For according to the Buddhist doctrine of momentariness and cause-effect, the present actually contains all the past. But this also actually puts it more within our power. For though we cannot bypass evil *karma* entirely, we can produce good present *karma* out of which will grow the future. What good we do now must inevitably bear its fruit or somewhat balance or compensate for the evil we have already done? Thus it is that Buddhism in its present mood of activism strongly accents in the inherent free will possessed by each man and the possibilities of improving both this life and his future lives' fortunes by present action. The very inevitability of *karmic* result enables the doer to depend upon the fruitage of his free deed. Therefore in current Buddhist usage *karma* is not so much a principle of consolation and explanation as a rousing call to be up and doing.

*Karma* has also become a bulwark of democracy and fellow-feeling, rather than the guarantor of priviledged position and autocracy. This transformation may be put in philosophical terms. *Karma* is only the individualised or personalised expression of the law of Dependent Origination. That is, each human being is only a group of psycho-physical elements conditioned by each other and having no existence or reality outside of that mutually conditioned existence. If there were not the body-factor there would be no mental factor, nor vice-versa, and of no human being. Usually this doctrine of Dependent Origination is used in connection with the *anātta* doctrine of the insubstantiality of the self to destroy the illusion of permanent self-hood.

But, in modern Buddhism, Dependent Origination is viewed "synthetically" by showing that all these phenomena are, in some way or other, conditionally related to each other. For some other interpreters, as the present Dalai Lama, this dependence means interdependence. Thus the individual who knows himself to be an entity whose "existence" is a case of Dependent Origination conditioned by the *karmic* law, and not of self-subsistent reality or independence. To be something in oneself is to be a part of every other self. This may be expressed, less philosophically, as the spirit of cooperation that springs out of the conviction that he who stands should take heed lest he fall. In this interpretation there is no technical violence to the doctrine itself. Even Nāgārjuna and Caṇdrakirti had reinterpreted the Law in their own fashion to suit the requirement of their times. And what the Dalai Lama has done in his interpretation is to lend a new life to the doctrine and the Law. There are similar cases in Christianity where, for example, the Calvinist doctrine of pre-destination became an immensely energising concept for a major strand of Protestant endeavour. Those who were persuaded that they had been predestined to victory under Divine purpose let nothing and no one withstand them in accomplishing that purpose in their lives.

We may turn to the concept of Bodhisattva. The concept is amply present in Theravāda no less. The concept entails the Buddha-vow, called *bodhi-citta*, i.e., to become a Buddha by endless lives of altruistic works. The current temperament of wishing to find in the tradition a more active social emphasis in bringing the *Bodhisattva* elements to the fore is gaining ground over the *arhat* ideal. The Bodhisattva is a self-sacrificing moral agent and volunteers to suffer the sufferings of others. It is significant that he recognises poverty as one of the aspects of *duhkha* as Śāntideva puts it in the *Bodhicaryāvatāra.* Hence the *Bodhisattva* vows to ameliorate the poverty of the poor and seeks out means (*upāya)* to do that. It is likely that the *Bodhisattva* ideal will be taken up, in lieu of *arhathood*, in Theravāda, and it will play a large part in the reorientation of orthodox Buddhism.

# 6

# In Search of a Social Ethics

We have been considering the somewhat instinctive reactions of those in the Buddhist tradition to the new social, cultural, and political factors in the contemporary world. These have been in the nature of adaptations of method, vocabulary, and general outlook in an attempt to meet current challenges to the Buddhist way of life and to make a large place for a Buddhist in world thought and life.

There have been attempts at a definite statement of Buddhist social and political principles applied to concrete situations. What could be the Buddhist reaction to communism? In India, a Buddhist and a Buddhist scholar of repute, Rahul Sankrityayana was a communist, rather a Marxist. Buddhism is known for its preference for the mean, the Middle Way. Can there be any Economics of the Middle Way? It is possible to a Buddhist and a socialist in political philosophy? In Myanmar independence leaders used communist ideology as a weapon against British control, and some of them were genuine Marxists to that end. Hence communism, as a species of socialism was not condemned in Myanmar until the sad events in Tibet.

Marxism and Buddhism agree on the denial of God, Soul, and purposive world-process. Buddhism would, of course, reject Marxist materialism; it stands for a mentalistic, rather than a materialistic, view of the world. Mind states determine physical states. Again Buddhism would disapprove class hatred and use of violence in class-struggle, it teaches harmony: *samavāya eva sādhu*. A Buddhist economy could be one which would moderate its plans. It will take a middle way. A Buddhist philosophy of economics would call for a moderation of those ambitious economic plans that would seek to make an enterprise or nation the biggest and best in the world, or aim at ever-expanding expansion and production. It would presumably limit personal wealth by means of taxes. And on the other hand, it would limit the lower range of income so that grinding poverty would be avoided or eliminated by state action.

Buddhism requires the freedom of the individual to determine his own destiny and choose the kind of life he lives. He must not be subordinated to group interests who seek to mould him to a standardised pattern. For this reason the Buddha opposed caste distinctions, seeing in them an attempt to confine people in a rigid framework and prevent the full realisation of their potentialities. Buddhism's essential democratic and egalitarian viewpoint finds expression in the Buddha's definition of caste in terms of the individual worth of a person, not in terms of an accident of birth. All four caste levels as well as women were adjudged capable of salvation. Even the vilest criminal has the potentiality for a complete transformation of personal character. This represents a somewhat new use of *karma* doctrine. Those hidden potentialities of *karmic* self are in a democratic content, to be developed, and apparently represent a precious heritage.

A Buddhist society is not a classless society because of these same *karmic* endowments which differentiate one man from another. As Ambedkar puts it, Buddhism is democratic, but makes no attempt to achieve a classless society. It classifies men according to their character and natural abilities. It is thus antithetical to a totalitarian concept. The question is: How does Buddhism understand the idea of competition? It would be competition without rivalry, for in victory of oneself does not mean the defeat of someone else. On the contrary, every spiritual victory to oneself is one that should and can be shared with all. The Buddhist finds no difficulty in conceiving himself as a citizen of the world, a member of the great brotherhood of mankind. He acknowledges his kinship with all that breathes, lives and hopes.

Buddhism would steer a middle course between capitalism and communism. Capitalism ensures four democratic freedoms: national, political, personal and economic. Communism encourages central planning, the stopping of uneconomic competition and the enthusiasm of the workers. Buddhism would avoid the extremes of these two economic methods and take the best from each. The specifics of the Middle Way suggest an economy within the limits of national resources. Extreme *laissez-faire* capitalism is to be avoided on one side, as is rigid state regimentation on the other. Every man must have some capital of his own if he is to be free and self-respecting, and there is to be true democracy. The state is to assist in this process by giving the poorer man an opportunity to receive the monetary results of his own labour by a system of just distribution.

The Middle Way may sound utopian, as do the hopes of many pioneers. The point is that in Buddhist societies political-economic versions of Buddhism are being formulated. It appears that socialism is the ideal Buddhist pattern. The Buddhist scriptures provide a considerable number of instances which show that Buddhism favours a welfare state in which the government has assumed responsibility for the care of the poor, the unemployed, the sick and the aged. The *Digha Nikāya* portrays the ideal kings as "fathers" of their people, caring for each subject as for a son. The Buddha had praised the government and the people of Vaishali for their republican mode of administration and living. The "kings" were elected. These rejection of the profit motive as a dangerous venom that poisons the well-springs of life in society which embodies it, for it enshrines greedy strife as a major "virtue". Capitalism in the modern sense would be condemned, root and branch, by Buddhism, and socialism would be welcomed as the perfect expression of the Buddhist economic way of life.

Buddhism and Socialism then as forms of society agree on the proper functions and goals of society. Buddhism, as religion, will supply the ideal pattern and the inspiration for the new state, while socialism provides the practical method of the implementation of the ideal. The question is: What could be the basic Buddhist reason for urging socialism. A socialist state or world would make it much easier to achieve the virtue of equanimity. The whole communal structure of mutual concern and sharing will itself serve to forward all men on their way to *nirvāṇic* realisation. The Socialist society will enshrine (a) right view with regard to property; (b) *Śīla, Samādhi, and Prajñā* will become dominant principles of life and (c) Communal charity will become possible and further people towards loving, sympathetic and compassionate to one another. The idealities of Buddhism and the practicalities of statecraft and realities of administration are of course not to be confused. Buddhism can also take care of that.

What future course Buddhist ethics will take? The course of development of a culture or religion is clear and inevitable only after it has taken place. What might seem to be the logic of its development is not bound to happen. Religious developments are seldom logical in terms of predictable results or inevitable effects following from specific doctrines or viewpoints. And in the present instance there are so many variable and unforceable factors, political, economic, social, personal—which will strongly affect the response that Buddhism will finally make to the new world situation.

Buddhism must make up its mind in which world it expects to live and strive, before it can give a clear answer to its ethical problems. For there are two worlds here with their respective values and ways: there is the world of absolute transcendent value (*nirvāṇa*) and the world of relative mundane concerns *(karma)*.

In the past there was a solution of sorts: it was held that though most men necessarily lived in the world of *karma*, they were really only marking time in it. For this lower world was neither worthy nor capable of salvation or whole-hearted concern. The temporal world is not to be saved. Contrast this attitude with that of the West: the world is worth saving, in all its complexities and particulars. If this world is to be perpetuated and perfected, it must still be this world. For Buddhism, there is nothing permanent in the physical or psychical, no lasting substance or enduring ego.

Now this is a fundamental matter about which Buddhism must make up its mind: Does it wish to live by the philosophy that the world is worth saving, and give to that saving a substantial effort by attempting the world's transformation for the better? Or does it wish to turn away to the higher world of transcendent inner values and largely ignore and deplore modern materialism and its civilisation which is firmly proceeding towards the goal of some sort of world betterment? Or can it find some way in which to combine the two in a new and dynamic synthesis? Obviously until Buddhism makes up its mind, or perhaps its heart, about the matter, no clear ethical philosophy or course of action can be charted.

There are factors tending towards all three solutions. The heavy traditional weight of Buddhism is with the second solution. Let the world go by; it is not worth saving, and is perhaps going to blow itself into pieces, in any case, a very drastic form of "betterment". The only salvation is retreat to inner peace. But there is also the prod of unhappy circumstances and socio-political disturbance that is increasingly invading this attempted seclusion.

The natural reaction of Buddhists is to try to combine the values of the interior and exterior worlds, the world of eternity and the world of time, in a viable synthesis. The general pattern which this synthesis takes as the rule: an activation of the *nirvāṇic* vocabulary and its application to concrete social situations in the form of the ideal of disinterested and unselfish but active endeavour. The contemporary Buddhist assertion is that *Nirvāṇa* and *Karma* can be reconciled both in ideal and action. The Buddha cannot be thought to be against social welfare but against indulgence in sensual desires. Achieving a better material standard of living, care for the poor and distressed, maintainance of social order is quite in keeping with the teachings of the Buddha. There can be no peace within when there is no peace without. But a question remains: Can a world-view that gives only negative approval or neutral consent to the promotion of social welfare, as a mere means for securing ultimate escape from the world of society, ever adequately deal with the aggressive counter-forces of contemporary world society? Can such a philosophy produce a social dynamism sufficient to create a vital new order: or will the *nirvāṇic* potency paralyse, or at least weaken, the vital nerve of active social involvement? It is impossible to answer such a question confidently, but the latter danger is present, whatever the final result.

We may turn to a second question: where will Buddhism find its leadership for the new day? Here again it is caught between its two worlds. The monk has been the moral and spiritual leader in the Buddhist world. The *Sangha* provided the wisdom to society. The *Sangha* leadership is now being bypassed. The way-farer on the path to *Nirvāṇa* is ignorant of the political-social world about him, cannot give Buddhism the leadership it needs in its day of crisis. Can the monk retain its leadership if he forsakes or modifies his traditional pattern of life and service? Buddhist sentiment is opposed to such modification and demands that he remains as he is, apart from, and above, all social welfare and political activity, the visible hope of *Nirvāṇa* for the common man.

Most people of this generation tend to put Buddhism in one compartment and socio-political in another compartment of their thinking and acting. A living synthesis of the two on the practical and effective plane scarcely seems to be a major concern among them. It is because their worlds are divided. One is of traditional, of the strictly personal sort, and the other is the world of present-day science, technology, politics, and economics. Nor is there yet a clear pattern for bringing them together.

But granted that something of significance will come from the new lay leaders: what will be the composition and quality of this new version of Buddhism? Undoubtedly, it will be of practical sort. Emphasis will be given to the value and efficacy of Buddhist doctrine and practice for every-day life. In any event, the tendency to over-value the personal and discount the systematic and technical seems to be the Achilles heel of all present Buddhist social-political philosophy and methodology.

One final item remains: what thought-forms or terms are likely to play the most significant role in any new formulation of Buddhist ethics in the tradition? Here again prediction is most difficult if not impossible. A religious tradition tends to express those values that its devotees desire it to express. Therefore to say with certainty that this term and not that one will play a basic role in new doctrinal formulation, or become the vehicle of new meanings which are being poured into it, is unprofitable. What we can say is that whatever occurs here, there will be no radically new formulations nor any wholesale discarding of old terms. It will be rather in the shift of emphasis or interpretation that novelty will make itself felt; and it will be under cover of reviving and rediscovering the ancient and original truth.

Certain terms seem capable of serving as the channels of the currents of change and revitalisation. *Karma* may be reinterpreted in terms of each man's power to change his future, both immediate and long-term. *Nirvāṇa* may be interpreted to mean a dispassionate, balanced quality of judgment brought to bear upon social situations and mundane problems. The *brahma-vihāras,* i.e., *maitrī, karuṇā, muditā* and upekṣā, may be given a more activist implementation than formerly. And the *Bodhisattva* ideal with its almost unlimited potentiality for social-service motivation, may spring into new importance, either implicit or explicit. But whether these potentialities will indeed be realised and revitalisation of Buddhist ethics be also realised through their instrumentality must remain the secret of Buddhism's unknown future.

# 7

# Buddhism and Society: Political Implications

*Dharma,* for Buddhism, is a means of enlightenment. The Buddha himself compares it to a raft. Just as a raft serves to cross over great stretches of water and then abandoned, so the *Dharma*, by means of which we ferry over the waters of birth and death to the other shore, *Nirvāṇa*, is not something to be taken with us but something to be left behind (*Majjhima – Nikāya,* I.134). In short, it is not an end in itself, but only a means to an end. In modern terminology, its function is purely instrumental and therefore its value only relative. This, of course, does not mean that it can be dispensed with. So long as we remain on this shore, or are still paddling across the stream, it is indispensable. The pragmatic nature of *Dharma* is emphasised in many a discourse of the Buddha.

The relation between Buddhism and politics is not quite simple. Buddhism comprises, from the institutional point of view, two groups, one large and one small, the first being the community of lay believers, both male and female, and the second, the noble Order of monks. These two groups need not have the same kind of relation to politics. In order to understand clearly the relation between Buddhism, both personal and institutional, on the one hand, and politics in the various senses of the term, on the other, it would be necessary to investigate the relations between (a) the Buddhist doctrine and political theories, (b) Buddhism and the State; (c) the laity and the government, (d) the *Sangha* and the government, (e) the layman and practical politics, and (f) the monk and practical politics.

We shall consider the points one by one:

(a) As far as our knowledge concerns, the Buddha confined his attention to questions of spiritual discipline, and refrained from making any pronouncement upon the relative merits of rival political theories and systems. During his time two types of government prevailed in north-eastern India, the monarchical and the republican, but the Buddha did not praise or condemn either. His statement that so long as the Vaijans, a conferacy of republican tribes, would assemble repeatedly and in large numbers, just so long their property might be looked for and not their decay, cannot be regarded as favouring republicanism (Digha-*Nikāya,* II.73). He merely stated facts of the case without passing any ethical judgment. On one point, however, the Buddha, and after him the entire Buddhist tradition was quite explicit: the government must uphold the moral and spiritual law being the means to enlightenment. Buddhism naturally demands that the state should recognise the fact that the true goal of life was to attain *nirvāṇa,* and that, therefore, it has the duty of providing for its citizens a political and social organisation within which both monks and the laity can live according to *Dharma*. Between Buddhism, on the one hand, and any political theory which recognises, either implicitly or explicitly, the supremacy of the moral and spiritual law and makes provision for its individual and collective application, on the other, there can be no disagreement. From the Buddha's social egalitarianism, as well as from his deliberate decentralisation of authority in the *Sangha*, it may be inferred that a form of government, in theory democratic, in effect aristocratic (for an intelligent electorate would naturally elect the best man), would be in accordance with his teaching. Buddhism has no objection to either a socialistic or to a capitalistic state provided it makes provision not only for the material, but also for the moral and spiritual well-being of its subjects.

(b) The nature of the relation between Buddhism and the State will vary in accordance with two factors, one being, of course, the nature of the State itself, the other, the relative strength of the Buddhist population. In a predominantly non-Buddhist state, Buddhism would expect to enjoy the same rights as other religious minorities. That is to say, it would demand complete freedom to practise and propagate its tenets, whether persecuted or tolerated, however, Buddhist citizens would always remain loyal to the State to which they belonged. In a predominantly Buddhist State, Buddhism would naturally expect official recognition as the state religion. Under democracy, the State is the people, and the government is only the agency through which the will of the people is carried out. If in their individual capacity the citizens support Buddhism it is only logical that they should do so in their collective capacity, too. Also, Buddhism being divided not into sects but schools, its recognition as the state religion is attended by no difficulty. In Sri Lanka, Myanmar, Kampuchia and Laos only Theravāda exists. In Mahāyāna lands, such as China and Japan, the laity in general respect and support all schools, and the state would do the same. Buddhist schools are tolerant, in fact, not only of each other, but also of non-Buddhist traditions.

(c) Not much indeed be said about the relation between the individual citizen and the government, because Buddhism has no means of enforcing among its adherents uniformity of action in the affairs of secular life. It is true that Buddhism does not only inculcate certain principles but also indicates the main lines of their application; the details of the application are left to be worked out by the individual Buddhist, each for himself. Buddhism exhorts, it does not command. It tells us, for example, that to take life is morally wrong; but it leaves us free to determine for ourselves whether the acceptance of this teaching obliges us to be a vegetarian or a conscientious objector. A

Buddhist, however, should take an active interest in whatever concerns the material, moral and spiritual well-being of his fellows-citizens. In short, it should be his endeavour to live his social and political life in accordance with the *Dharma*.

(d) The relation of the Government to the *Sangha* is the same as that of the individual by Buddhist to the individual *bhikṛu.* The relation of the *Sangha* to the Government corresponds to the relation between the *bhikṣu* and the layman. Just as the monk, in his capacity of guide, philosopher and friend, indicates to the lay devotee the path of righteousness, so it is the right and duty of the *Sangha,* in the person of its seniormost members, to advise the government not only on the propagation of *Dharma* but also on its application to the social and political life of the nation. The *Sangha* must also be able to draw attention to and freely criticise deviations from the *Dharma* on the part of the government, the people, and the political leaders. Unless the *Dharma* is applied to the national life, it will loose its hold over domestic life. Being concerned with the preservation of the *Dharma,* the *Sangha* is inevitably concerned with its application also, whether, to politics or any other sphere of life. Needless to add that the advice of the *Sangha* should never tend to the promotion of anything, but peace and prosperity are both at home and abroad. Whoever the *Sangha* spoke to, it would have but one message: "Never in this world does hatred cease by hatred: it ceases only by love. This is the Law Eternal." (*Dhammapada*, 5).

(e) The individual monk should have no relation with the government as government except through the Sangha, or with the consent of the *Sangha.* Unless there happens to be a separate portfolio for religious affairs, or a special provision for ecclesiastical councilors, as there is in Thailand, he should not accept any office in the government, and even in such cases as these he should not accept any remuneration. A monk cannot be required to undertake any form of national service; neither is he liable to conscription. In a Buddhist State these rights would be recognised automatically.

(f) Since the Buddhist layman is connected with the government, he is obviously to take part in practical politics, and all that can usefully be said in this connection is that here, too, he should act in accordance with the *Dharma.*

(g) The monk, however, is under no such obligation. On the contrary, by virtue of the rules which, at the time of his ordination, he undertakes faithfully to observe, he is obliged to refrain from participation in practical politics. The monk is not to support or join or even vote for, any political organisation. Neither should he participate in meetings or any other public functions of a political or quasi-political nature. For those members of the *Sangha* who feel, as some of Myanmar and Sri Lanka have felt in recent times, that their duties as citizens have a stronger claim on them than their obligations as monk, the only honourable course is to leave the *Sangha.* Enlightenment and elections cannot be won together.

Hardly less striking is the almost invariable association of Buddhism with peace. Not a single page of Buddhist history has even been lurid with the light of inquisitional fires, or darkened with the smoke of heretic cities ablaze, or red with the blood of the guiltless victims of religious hatred. Like the Bodhisattva Manjuśrī, Buddhism wields only the sword of wisdom, and recognises only one enemy, Ignorance. This is the testimony of history, and is not to be gainsaid.

But even admitting the close association of Buddhism with place in Asia it may be questioned whether Buddhism was really the cause and peace the effect. Perhaps their association was fortuitous, Buddhism has a bloodless and Christianity a bloody record, it might be argued, not so much because of any difference between their teachings but because one has propagated among the warlike tribes of Western Europe and the other among the peaceable nations of Asia. The contention is unfounded. Tibet before the introduction of Buddhism, was the greatest military power in Asia. The early history of Myanmar, Cambodia and Thailand shows that the people of those countries were originally of an extremely warlike, even aggressive in disposition. The Mongol hordes at one time overran not only the whole of Central Asia, but also India, China, Persia and Afghanistan, and thundered even at the gates of Europe. China exhibited at various periods of her history considerable military activity. The material spirit of Japan is far from being subdued after nearly fifteen centuries of Buddhism. With the possible exceptions of India and China, the nations of Asia were originally no less pugnacious and predatory than those of Europe. Their subsequent peacefulness was due very largely to the pacific teachings of Buddhism. But one hardly expects to be able to pacify turbulent and warlike nations by preaching to them a God of Battles. It may, therefore, be concluded that the association between Buddhism and peace is not fortuitous but inevitable. Buddhism has been in the past, is at present, and will continue to be in future, a factor contributing to the establishment of universal peace.

From what has been said above, it should already be clear that in the present, no less than in the past, Buddhism implies peace. But this peace is not a condition of unstable political equilibrium but rather a state of mind purified from all feelings of antagonism and thoroughly permeated by that impersonal and universal love, which the Buddhists call, *maitrī*. Buddhism works from within outwards. Its hierarchy enjoys no international diplomatic status, and chooses to act not by means of behind–the–scenes political wire–pulling but by the open practice end propagation of the pacific teachings of the Buddha. On the political plane, Buddhism does not take sides. Love, in the sense of *maitrī,* is the most powerful force in the world; but it is a natural force. Whether one's love be directed towards concrete persons and things, or whether it be directed towards abstract conceptions and ideals, if it causes one to feel hatred towards some other object, of a different kind, it is of a limited extent, and therefore, not true love but only a species of attachment. Similarly, if peace, which is a form of love, is not universal it is not peace at all. The conclusion of a private peace between two or more nations, to the exclusion of the remainder, is in reality impossible. Should such a "peace" in any way threaten the security of any other state, even its observance would be on no higher a moral plane than the honesty that is popularly supposed to exist among thieves. India having accepted Aśoka's great ideal of *dharmavijaya* or conquest by Righteousness, it was inevitable that this very Buddhist *maitrī*, or love and goodwill towards all, should form the ultimate spiritual basis of her policy of dynamic neutrality in world affairs. It is the *raison d'etre* of the fact that, while working unremittingly for world peace, the Government of India consistently refuses to align itself with any power bloc. Such an attitude has naturally drawn her closer to the Buddhist countries of South-East Asia, whose respective policies are naturally inspired by one and the same ideal. But by its very nature, such a relationship does not and cannot imply hostility or even indifference towards any other country or group of countries. In fact, it is not one political group among other groups, with its own exclusive preferences and limited loyalties, but rather a slowly expanding centre radiating to the world the impersonal, universal and neutral power of *maitrī.* It is in this light that one must view the Government of India's attempts to renew her ancient ties with the countries of Asia. It is because Buddhism alone can provide the necessary basis for these attempts that its political implications for Asia, and through Asia for the whole world, are so enormous and so important.

Buddhism has remained a cultural force in Europe, and Russell has gone so far as to declare that if he were compelled to choose between the religions of the world he would choose Buddhism. We may recall that Schopenhauer, in the second decade of the nineteenth century, had declared himself a Buddhist, and following him Nietzsche, and still later Wittgenstein have become intellectual forces looking back to Buddhism, and motivating what now goes under the banner of postmodernism.

But more importantly, let us not forget that the Buddha aimed at the development of a new type of freemen, free from prejudices, intent on working out his own future, with reliance on one' own self, *ātmadīpa*. As Radhakrishnan has pointed out that the Buddha is an outstanding representative of our religious tradition, and his teachings have become integral part of our culture. In a sense, says Radhakrishnan, the Buddha is a maker of modern Hinduism (*2500 Years of Buddhism*, p. xvi, The Publications Division, New Delhi, 1959).

The Buddha's humanism had crossed racial and national barriers. Yet the chaotic condition of world affairs reflects the chaos in man's souls. History has become universal in spirit. Its subject matter is neither Europe nor Asia, neither East nor West, but humanity in all lands and ages. In spite of political divisions, the world is one, whether we like it or not. The fortunes of everyone are linked up with those of others. But we are suffering from an exhaustion of spirit, an increase of egoism, individual and collective, which seem to make the ideal of a world society too difficult to desire. What we need today is a spiritual view of the universe. We must recover the lost ideal of spiritual freedom *ātmalābhan na param vidyate.* If we wish to achieve peace we must maintain that inner harmony, that poise of soul, which are the essential elements of peace. We must possess ourselves even though all else is lost. The free spirit sets no bounds to its love, recognises in all human beings a spark of holiness, and offers itself up as a willing victim to the cause of mankind. It casts off all fear except that of wrong doing, passes the bounds of time and death and finds inexhaustible power in life eternal. Let us not forget that Buddhism is a religion of kindness, humanity and equality.

# 8

# The Resurgence of the Bodhisattva Ideal

## I

### The Resurgence of the Bodhisattva Ideal in Recent Indian Thought

The term 'recent' spans centuries, and overlaps with 'modern' in the sense that Descartes is held as a modern philosopher. In Indian context, 'recent' and 'modern' maps the new age that dawned in the nineteenth century, in the wake of British system of education and revaluation of the medieval values and ways of life. There has been the problem with Buddhism in so far as our cultural attitude and beliefs concerning the Buddha's teachings of the Way. Historically the disappearance of Buddhism from the Indian scene has been a problem issue with the general trend of Hindu ideal of life and practice. Hindu mind has always been uncomfortable with the Buddhist thesis of *anātmavāda*, and *kṣanabhangavāda*. These two have been the points of attack by non-Buddhist schools. Udayana wrote the *Ātmatattvaviveka* with the sole intention of refuting the Buddhist thesis of *anātma* or *niḥsvabhāvatā*. Kumārila's tirade against Buddhism took the form of a frontal attack in the *Bauddhadhikkāra*. But Kumārila had respect for Buddhist ethics. He had the honesty to admit that the Buddhist code of conduct emphasing *ahimsā* is a noble one, though its repudiation of the Vedas is ignoble. For Kumārila, the truth of Buddhism is mixed up with much that is false, and so he compares it to the milk put in the dog's skin, *Śvācarmanikṣipta kṣiravad* (*Tantravārttika*, 1.3.6). Usually Śaṁkara is credited with routing Buddhism out of India. But this is a stupid and ignorant notion. In the *Brahmasūtra bhāṣya*, Śaṁkara had argued against a good many philosophical schools like Vaiśeṣika, Sāṁkhya, Jainism, the Pāśupat and Pañcaratra views, besides a couple of shades of Buddhism, comprising the Vaibhāṣika, Sautāntrika and Vijñānavāda. The Buddhist schools apart, the schools and the views rebutted by Śaṁkara have been thriving as before. But why should the disappearance of Buddhism is ascribed to Śaṁkara's critique of it? Philosophical wrangling can never the cause of the disappearance of any school. There must have been historical reasons of which Hindu culture and philosophy remains gleefully ignorant and indifferent to. Many would say that Kumārila critiqued Buddhism, but no one mentions that Śāntarakṣita gave a fitting reply to Kumārila in *Tattvasaṁgraha*. The older school of the Nyāya had Buddhism as its chief philosophical opponent or *pūrva pakṣa*, while the later development of Nyāya had the Mimāṁsaka as the major contender. This change is significant historically. In our times, Daya Krishna has raised the question urging philosophers to look into the causes of the change of philosophical climate. The Brāhminical line of thinking felt unformatable with the Buddhist mode of metaphysical thinking. To some it appeared that the Buddhists lacked philosophical or metaphysical depth. Vivekananda, for example, remarked that the Buddhist thought was lacking in metaphysics. He said, "I do not endorse all his philosophy. I want a good deal of metaphysics for myself" (*Selections* from Vivekananda, p. 361, Advaita Ashram, Kolkata, 2007). It appears that Vivekananda had Pali Buddhism in mind when he made the remark, for Sanskrit Buddhism, or Mahāyāna in particular, is quite sophisticated an affair in the matter of metaphysical depth and probing. A perusal of his writings reveals to us that Vivekananda had never encountered Nāgārjuna's or Candrakirṭi's dialectical writings. In one of his lectures Vivekananda touches the Vijñānavāda thesis of momentariness of consciousness, but that closely follows Śaṁkara's footsteps, in taking side with the Advaita response to the Buddhist point of view. But there can be no doubt about the fact that Vivekananda had unbounded regard and respect for the Buddha, and he had been a great admirer of the ethical excellence that the Buddha embodied. For Vivekananda, the Buddha stood for the great ethical ideal, absolutely disinterested altruism, and he appropriated the Buddha's classic call to work for the good and happiness of the many in his own missionary agenda.

There has been ambivalence on the part of our cultural leaders, and this consists in separating the person of the Buddha from his teachings. His teachings had made the sensibility of the followers of the Brāhminical lineage of culture and life somewhat uncomfortable. So the Buddha's moral personality is held in high esteem, while casting his teachings away. There is a notable feature amongst our modern thinkers. What could be the reason for the ambivalence?

Radhakrishnan touched upon this issue with the remark that it is not true that Buddhism have left no trace in the lineage of Indian philosophical thinking. The alleged disappearance is to be understood as having gone sub-terrainian. The best and noble elements of the Buddhist heritage have been absorbed into the Hindu way of life and culture. Of our recent thinkers, Radhakrishnan alone paid a greater attention to the Buddhist thought in his writings. He translated the *Dhammapada* with a commentary, lectured on the Buddha in the Master Mind series to the British Academy, and above all, the masterful discussion on Vijñānavāda and Nāgārjuna in the first volume of *Indian Philosophy*.

The point is that there has been a conscious endeavour at accommodating the Buddha and his teachings as a valued integral part of the Indian heritage. Tilak, for instance, devoted a section on the Buddha and the Pali Buddhist philosophical writings in his celebrated commentary on the *Gītā*. The trend continued through such other important thinkers like Rabindranath Tagore and Sri Aurobindo.

Let us take the case of Rabindranath Tagore. He was born in a family that espoused the beliefs of reformed Hindu Church, the Brāhmo Samaj, founded by Rammohan Ray. Rabindranath's father, Debendranath was the leader of the church, and compiled its scripture, the *Brāhmadharma*. It has selections of non-idolatrous, and non-advaitic passages from the Upaniṣad, and no less importantly from the *Dhammapada*, besides such works as the *Mahābhārata* and the *Mahānirvāṇa Tantra*, etc. Rabindranath, all through his life put *Upaniṣad* on the same pedestal in the company of the *Dhammapada*. He looked upon the both as forming one unbroken spiritual inheritance through history. This was a matter of the spirit, and for Rabindranath there was no Brāhminical-Buddhist divide.

Rabindranath was drawn towards such Buddhist values as *maitrī* and the ideal of *Brahmavihāra*. He wrote an essay in explication of the metaphor of the mother in the *Metta Sūtta* of the *Sūtta Nipāta.* It was for him the great moral ideal to be inculcated in society. He was one of the pioneers of Buddhist studies and invited scholars to translate and write on the Buddhist moral ideas at the centre he founded in Santineketan. He travelled to Buddhist countries and noticed how Buddhism helped the flourishing of art and culture wherever it was taken to. As for his contribution to the spread of Buddhism in the domain of culture he wrote poems and dramas on Buddhist themes, and these stand to attest both his creative genius as a literary artist as well as his unfailing admiration for the Buddha and his compassionate teachings.

Vivekananda regarded the Buddha as the highest point of man's spiritual evolution. He called it "the Buddha-man", "the greatest man that was ever born" (*Selections from Vivekananda*, p. 53, and other entries under Buddha and Buddhism). Vivekananda took the Buddha standing as "the perfection of the active type" (*ibid.* p. 362) and he wished if he "had one infinitesimal part of Buddha's heart". He even went to the extent of saying that Buddha was his *ishta*. On this point a portion of his letter (dated February, 1890) is worth quoting: "Lord Budddha is my Ishta-my God. He preached no theory about Godhead-he was himself God, I fully believe it". (*Letter*-12, p.19, Adwaita Ashram, Kolkata, 2008). This is a remarkable statement hardly ever taken note of. Yet apart from his personal adoration of the Buddha, Vivekananda considered the social element of Buddhism to be the most unique. The Buddha's deep all-embracing humanism was at the root of his practice of *brahma-vihāra*. Vivekananda referred to it as "the Buddha's heart": "that sympathy, that love, that heart, that thinks for all, until Buddha's heart comes once more into India...., there is no hope for us" (*Selections*, p. 273). And as for the relationship of Buddhism to Hinduism, Vivekananda had no qualms about the fact that the Buddha was "the fulfilment, the logical conclusion, the logical development of the religion of the Hindus", and again, "The separation between the Buddhists and the Brahmins is the cause of the downfall of India" (*ibid,* pp. 16-17).

This Buddhology, as envisaged and formulated so passionately by Vivekananda reappears in Sri Aurobindo's evolutionary philosophy. In *The Life Divine*, Sri Aurobindo distinguishes between the two poises of Brahman, silent and active. Silence and Activity flow into each other, and Sri Aurobindo takes the case of the Buddha as exemplifying the modalities of the Real, and says, "Thus was it possible for the Buddha to attain the state of *Nirvaṇa* and yet act puissantly in the world, impersonal in his inner consciousness, in his action the most powerful personality that we know of as having lived and produced results upon earth" (*The Life Divine*, New York, 1949, pp. 29-30). Again, later in that work Sri Aurobindo formulates his ideal of the gnostic being. The concept of 'gnostic being' tolls back to the Mahāyana ideal of Bodhisattva. In the life of the gnostic being, there is "a close and complete consciousness of the self of others, a consciousness of their mind, life, physical being which are felt as if they were one's own. The gnostic being will act, not out of a surface sentiment of love and sympathy or any similar feeling, but out of this close mutual consciousness, this intimate oneness" (*ibid.* p. 913). Anyone familiar with Śāntideva's *Bodhicaryāvatāra* would at once recall the twin processes of *parātma samatā* and *parātma parivartana* requisite for the bodhisattva to act for the good of others. The moral agent has to realise his oneness (*samatā*) with others who are in suffering and need help. In the process the bodhisattva transforms (*parivartana*) his self into the self of others. The point is that unqualified spontaneous altruism becomes possible only the twin metaphysical processes. (See *Bodhicaryāvatāra*, Chapter VIII, Verse 137-139).

There can be no doubt as regards the foundational experience for motivelessness of altruism to be possible at all looks back the Buddhist formulation as indicated above. In some form or other, all the leaders of recent Indian thought have spelled their views and theories around the basic Buddhist insight. Sri Aurobindo has been the first ever to point to this chain of the ideal. The spiritually realised, the liberated man is preoccupied with the good of all beings; Buddha discovering the way of *Nirvāṇa* must turn back to open that way to those who are still under the delusion of their constructive instead of their real being—or non-being; Vivekananda, drawn by the Absolute, feels also the call of the disguised Godhead in humanity and most the call of the fallen and the suffering, the call of the self to the self in the obscure body of the universe" (*ibid,* pp. 930-31). How are we explain or understand the linkage: the Buddha, Vivekananda and Sri Aurobindo's conception of the gnostic being. There can be no doubt that it is in point of fact a resurgence of the bodhisattva ideal in our own times.

Let us connect three assertions to this effect. There is first one quote from Rabindranath Tagore: "If the world passes on in tears how could I sit alone pursuing my own salvation?" Vivekananda wrote to his brother monks: "Of what consequence is it to the world if I on or I attain mukti? We have to take the whole world to mukti". The Dalai Lama, who is avowedly a follower of the *Bodhisattva yāna*, has told to Claude B. Levenson: "I, for the greater good of living being, I had to be reincarnated as, say a bridge or an insect, as a monk who follows the Mahāyāna it is my duty to do it. As long as there are beings who suffer, I shall return". (*The Dalai Lama*, p. 272, Oxford University Press, 2006). The bodhisattva lives and dies for others. The ideal has stood out through centuries as a paradigm of moral perfection. The jīvanmukta may live for others, but does not die for them. Altruism is the *raison d'etre* of a bodhisattva's existence. In India, it was Appayya Dikṣita who adumbrated the ideal of *sarvamukti*, as the logical goal of Vedāntic ethical development. For him, *sarvamukti* was theological necessity, an implication for *eka-jīva-vāda*, the doctrine of the unity of all *jīvas*. It suggests that there is only one *jīva*. However, Appayya Dikṣita did not get a hearing from the orthodox Vedāntins. For them, *mukti* was a solitary ritual. On the other hand, the details of the bodhisattva ideal had changed, interpretations had differed, certain ideas had evolved, others lost in importance, refinements were made in the stages of the path. It was a dynamic, living ideal. And at the hands of recent Indian thinkers, the ideal has been adapted to modern needs. The heart of the ideal, its essence, has remained the same. It has received a new life, new expression and new authority through writings of the thinkers we have mentioned above. We may add further that Gandhi's concept of *sarvodaya* obviously bears the streaks of bodhisattva inspiration. His idea of Truth, as the unity of all living beings, implies the ethics of non-violence.

## II

### Engaged Buddhism: Social and Political Visions of Ambedkar's Neo-Buddhism

We shall now turn to a more recent phenomenon of Buddhist socio-political movement as led by Ambedkar, for which the grounds were prepared by the thinkers and their ideas in theoretical form.

Like all religions Buddhism has experienced reform movements throughout history to restore the original core values of the faith when leadership and institutions have fallen into decay. Korea, Japan, Thailand and Sri Lanka, Myanmar, and India have not been exceptions to the general statement. Modern Buddhism in Asia is not just a meditative vehicle for spiritual liberation, but is now also a vehicle that includes liberation movements for social and political change. What has come to be known as "socially engaged Buddhism" or simply "engaged Buddhism" is a vast array of Asian movements, dedicated to addressing the economic, social, political and environmental as well as the spiritual needs of modern humankind. For example, in South-East Asia Buddhist monks work with lay volunteers to rejuvenate village life. In South Asia Indian untouchables have converted to form a Buddhist movement for social change and put an end to the misery of caste system. In East Asia Buddhist lay movements have drawn millions of members by caring for their daily needs. And throughout Asia, Buddhist nuns are founding orders that work for institutional changes in the Buddhist monastic communities and organise social, educational, and health services for the poor. And, their response to this situation is not only to help people practice spirituality for the sake of personal liberation, but also to change the economic system for the sake of social liberation. The Buddhist ideal encouraged positive activities. Ambedkar's admonition is there on record. He urged his disciples to go out and serve the people in the amelioration of their lot. The phrase of his admonition is famously well-known: *vahujana hitāya, vahujana sukhāya*. The great Buddhist king Aśoka in the Buddhist history (268-233 BCE) represents a model Buddhist ruler who always had his subject's economic and social well-being as his main concerns, and the great Indian philosopher Nāgārjuna advised a king (see *Ratnāvali*, 231-321) to govern with a compassionate socialism that included education for the people, fixed charges for doctors, socially supported healthcare, and low taxes. Engaged Buddhism has its meaning in the reconstructive prospects, based on the Buddha's method of deconstruction, for all sentient beings.

In Asia people look forward to reconstructing their identity as Buddhists with the correct Buddhism socially.

Ambedkar came to Buddhism through his critique of Hinduism formulated in terms of the social stratification based on caste systems. His general stand was that a people and their religion must be judged by social standards based on social ethics. He was of the opinion that religions are for the society and not society for religion. But what were Ambedkar's reasons for choosing Buddhism? In *The Buddha and His Dhamma* he has highlighted the features of Buddhism as follows:

1. Buddhism emphasised the role of reason as against faith or superstition.
2. Buddhism rejected many objects of dogmatic belief such as God and soul (Book IV, Part I).
3. Buddhism was opposed to caste system (Book III, Part V, Section 4).
4. Buddhism emphasised morality as an essence of good life. Morality in Buddhism is essentially human-centric and had no reference to soul and God (Book IV, Part I, Section 5).

Thus it was the rational, secular, moral and egalitarian aspects of Buddhism.

Ambedkar argued for reinterpreting Buddhism, since in spite of there being many progressive elements, egalitarian, secular and rational, these are not stated consistently and coherently, but are mixed with many regressive elements, such as rebirth and re-death, higher and lower worlds, etc. Buddhism comes down to us with myths and superstitions. The idea of suffering as a noble truth did not appeal to Ambedkar. According to him the element of pessimism is an undesirable element. He thought that Buddhism has a social message. The monks were urged by the Buddha to strive for the well-being and happiness of the many. He was disappointed to observe how the monks cared more for their personal liberation. Ambedkar wanted the monks to play a social role as missionaries and social workers. And lastly, he disapproved the division of Buddhism into various sects like Theravāda and Mahāyāna. He was inclined towards Theravāda for its realist ontology and morality in its approach to values. He sought to combine the best elements of Theravāda and Mahāyāna. He appreciated the Mahāyāna doctrine of *pāramitās* with emphasis on *prajñā* and *karuṇā* in his interpretation and reconstruction of Buddhism.

Ambedkara offered an alternative explanation of the Buddha's renunciation. He was influenced by Dharmananda Kosambi's researches in Pali Buddhism. The historical background of Siddarth's developing detachment and disinclination towards worldly life is the conflicts between Sākya and Koliya clans on the issue of sharing the water of the river Rohini. Seeing that people constantly fighting with each other, Gotama developed detachment and disinclination towards the life in the world. Further Ambedkar tries to show that the so called suffering pervading the whole of human life was in fact the suffering which arises out of one's social existence involving conflicts, inequality and injustices that bothered Gotama. In the light of Ambedkara's interpretation one can say that though Gotama's disenchantment with the worldly life was occasioned by Sākhya-Koliya war, he generalised this phenomenon of war into the general problem of conflict including in it even class struggle and caste struggle.

The important aspect of Ambedkar's interpretations of the Buddha's life is its demythologised characters. Adale Ficke and Christoph Emmridh have shown in their researches that Ambedkar sought to interpret was Buddhist scriptures to project the Buddha as a social reformer. (See S. Jondhale and Johames Beltz, *Reconstructing the World: B.R. Ambedkar and Buddhism in India*, Oxford University Press, New Delhi, 2004).

As for the pessimism of the teaching of the four Noble Truths, Ambedkar seeks to give an optimistic interpretation of the doctrine of suffering. He rejects the traditional interpretation, and suggests a realistic and empirical line of approach in lieu of the usual transcendental-metaphysical approach. So he restated the doctrine leaving room for hope and optimism, to show that a happy life in this world is indeed possible. Instead of saying that the world is of the nature of suffering, Ambedkar says that there is suffering in the world. Now the problem of suffering becomes the problem of removing the suffering from the world and not that of running away from the world itself. As he says, the world is full of suffering, but how to remove the suffering from the world is the only purpose of Dhamma.

There is more to Ambedkar's reconstruction of the traditional view of the doctrine of suffering, but these need not detain us. On the contrary, we propose to concentrate on the following elements of his reconstruction:

(a) The path of purity. He calls them the five "principles of life", the five-fold *śīla.*

(b) Under the title "The Doctrine of Virtue", Ambedkar includes the Mahāyāna doctrine of the *pāramitās,* or the states of perfection in virtues with emphasis on *prajñā-pāramitā*. There is a great emphasis on morality in Ambedkar's understanding of Buddhism. And morality, in traditional Buddhism is represented by *śīla*. This could be the reason why he thought that *śīla* was central theme in the Buddha's first sermon.

In the Mahāyāna lineage it is held that not one, but three *dharmacakra* sermons were delivered by the Buddha. The first sermon enunciates the doctrine of suffering, the second formulates the doctrine of *pāramitās*, and the third and the final one develop the doctrine of *vijñānavāda*. Ambedkar clubs the first and the second sermons together and holds that the doctrine of *pāramitās* was the theme the first sermon itself.

Dhamma is the second of the three jewels of Buddhism. Ambedkar's conception is an important part of his reconstruction of Buddhism. In simple terms, he identifies *dhamma* with morality and tries to remove various misconceptions. In Sanskrit, the word dharma is a polyguous term, and is popularly taken to mean religion. Does the Pali word *dhamma* share the same characteristic? Ambedkar denies the possibility in absolute terms. He tries to eliminate the traditional doctrines of karma and rebirth and presents a secular this worldly formulation of Buddhism. He is averse to associating Buddhism with any kind of transcendence or other worldliness.

Ambedkar contradistinguishes the Buddha's *dhamma* from other religions. In most religious belief in transcendental entities like God, soul and other worlds become the basis of morality. There operates the idea of morality as divine commandment. In interpreting Buddhism, Ambedkar makes morality the root of religion. Morality is the essence of the *dhamma*. Ambedkar reconstructs Buddhism in such a manner as by placing morality at the centre, while religious beliefs are made to rotate around it. The notions of karma and rebirth are mutually linked up and suggest a trans-empirical import. Ambedkar delinked the issues and restated then differently. He found the two doctrines inconsistent with the Buddhist view of *anātmavāda*, i.e., the denial of a continuous or constant identity of the moral agent. He denied the karma doctrine as it was traditionally understood and reinterpreted it in such a way that it no more implies the usual notion of rebirth. Ambedkar denied rebirth if it meant rebirth of a soul or rebirth of the same person. He understands death and rebirth in physical terms, he made the doctrine of rebirth independent of the doctrine of karma and rendered it morally neutral.

We may now turn to considering Ambedkar's justification of *dhamma*.

If *dhamma* is morality, and if this morality is not justified either on God's command, or on the basis of the doctrine of karma, or rebirth, then what is the *dhamma*-morality itself? Now Ambedkar is not a deontologist like Kant, so we may not say that for him morality is intrinsically justified. It appears that Ambedkar is a sort of consequentialist. The upholders of karma doctrine were also consequentialists. They hold that moral actions are to be performed keeping in mind their consequences to be borne by the agent. Ambedkar holds that morally good actions are to be performed for their consequences on the humanity at large. "Do *kuśala karma* so that humanity may benefit by a good moral order which a *kuśala karma* helps to sustain, do not do *akuśala karma* for humanity will suffer from bad moral order which an *akuśala karma* will bring about" (*The Buddha and His Dhamma*, III. VI. 25). This view may be called universal consequentialism. This morality is not transcendental. *Dhamma*, for Ambedkar's interpretation is a secular way of life based on morality, which aims at well-being of the whole humanity. Hence *dhamma* being secular morality is distinguished from the way of life based on belief in any supernatural power like God or ritual potency, nor is it rooted in speculative metaphysics or blind faith in some scriptures. One may develop freedom from passions and craving by realising the impermanence of all things and attain moral perfection.

Ambedkar identifies the category of *saddhamma* with the Buddha's teaching, and it forms an important part of his reconstruction of Buddhism. *Saddhamma* is alternatively called philosophy of Dhamma. It may be noted that Ambedkar uses the term 'philosophy' for a total social perspective, or we may call it his sociology of religion.

*Dhamma* refers initially to an individually moral perspective. Then the individual perspective becomes a social phenomenon by taking on dimension of moral relationships among all the members of the society. This is what Ambedkar calls *saddhamma*.

According to Ambedkar the social moral perspective of Buddhism consists of the principles like *prajñā, maitrī* and *karuṇā*. *Prajñā* in traditional Buddhism refers to wisdom concerning impermanence of whatever that exists, and the *anattā* doctrine. But Ambedkar gives it a more general form to include knowledge in general and learning which is to be made available to all. Ambedkar holds that over and above *prajñā*, *karuṇā* and *maitrī* are equally important as the part of *saddhamma.* He made the social reformation by way of eradicating caste-*varṇa* barriers and advocating equality an important part of *saddhamma. Dhamma* becomes *saddhamma* when individual moral pursuits of the people contribute to the general social good, which, in turn, leads to the establishment of an ideal society based on perfect justice. For Ambedkar the religion of the Buddha is perfect justice springing from a man's own meritorious disposition.

Ambedkar's notion of ideal society deserves a few words of clarification. The three principles of liberty, equality and fraternity constitute the core of Ambedkar's social philosophy. These very principles are the parameters of any ideal religion as well. Ambedkar does not exempt the Buddhist monks from his reconstruction. Traditionally, a *bhikku* of the Buddhist order was supposed to devote himself to disciplining his own behaviour, speech and mind by following the rules of *Śīla* and meditation. But Ambedkar wishes the monk to play the social role of spreading the understanding of *Dhamma* among the common people, and enlightening on the matters of morality. He found that the monks of Theravād countries like Śri Lanka and elsewhere were not playing their social role properly.

A *bhikku*, for Ambedkar is not an ascetic or recluse. He, according to Ambedkar, would fail as a *bhikku* if he is indifferent to the woes of the mankind. He should be a warrior, who does not avoid fighting when virtue is in danger.

We have thus far tried to follow Ambedkar in his project of reconstructing classical Buddhism. Now it is time to ask and see the reconstruction with reference to the question of the identity of Buddhism as a religion vis-a-vis the reform proposed by Ambedkar. The question may be asked at two levels:

(a) Can the reform proposed be justified in principle?

(b) What is the core of Buddhism? Does the reconstruction retain the core?

As the methodological issue of justifiability of the reform we have to see whether it is correct and we may note the following. In the Indian tradition philosophical innovations are not altogether a novel affair. Philosophical systems have evolved through new commentaries. In the context of Buddhist discourse proponents of various sects had considered some tenets as the core and others as peripheral, and accordingly rearranged and reinterpreted the Buddha's statements. Even the celebrated doctrine of four *Noble Truths* was criticised and deconstructed in Mādhyamika Buddhism. Hence Ambedkar's critique of the doctrine need not be looked upon as something sacrilegious or unusual.

Again, there is something anthropocentric, pragmatic and positivistic about Ambedkar's notion of religion. Religions are not revealed but natural. Religions have emerged in human societies in different times at different stages of civilisation. For Ambedkar, the function of religion is to sustain the social life of the people by the postulates and sanction of morality. He adds certain conditions to qualify any religion as ideals:

(i) A religion should be in accordance with science;

(ii) A religion must recognise the fundamental tenets of Liberty, Equality and fraternity;

(iii) A religion should not sanctify or ennoble poverty.

As and when a religion fails to fulfil the above requirements and fails to perform the role assigned to it, it stands in need of reform. It has to be reshaped in such a way that it performs its proper role.

Apropos of the project of reconstruction and reform it may be necessary to abandon a religion, to be converted to a more promising religion, to found a new religion or to reconstruct and refine the same old religion. Ambedkar abandoned Hinduism, and embraced Buddhism, not in its traditional form, but reformed and reshaped it. He called it Neo-Buddhism. It is non-identical with Hinayāna or Mahāyāna, but, as he claimed, is the authentic original Buddhism. The claim that Ambedkar made in his *The Buddha and His Dhamma* has been debated since the publication of the book in 1959.

Christopher Queen in studying Ambedkar's book locates it on the map of what he calls engaged Buddhism, i.e., social application of Buddhism represented earlier by many leaders of thought such as Henry Olcott, Anagarika Dhammapal and Buddhadāsa Bhikku. Accordingly, Ambedkar's reconstruction of Buddhism has to be considered as a part of the global social movement towards revitalisation and modernisation of Buddhism. Ambedkar's Buddhism retains the core of Theravāda tradition in the form of *Śīla* and *samādhi.* He also retains the Mahāyāna tradition, the core *pāramitās* of *prajñā* and *karuṇā*, which assume the form of education and science on the one hand, and social ethics and political reform, on the other.

Gail Omvelt's book *Buddhism in India: Challenging Brāhmanism and Caste* makes an important contribution on the issue of justification of Ambedkar's version of Buddhism. Her stand is that Ambedkar's form of Buddhism is engaged Buddhism or applied Buddhism. Grace Burford, a contemporary Indologist, has argued in *Desire, Death and Goodness: The Conflict of Ultimate Values in Theravāda Buddhism* (Peter Long, New York, 1991) that there is a conflict of ultimate values in the Theravāda tradition.

The Pali text *Atthakavagga* of the *Sūtta Nipāta* describes the good of life in terms of this-worldly, immanent and life-affirming value system. She argues that the true classical Buddhism is life-affirming, the escape from the birth and death round is a peripheral preoccupation. By referring to Burford's argument we may claim along with Gail Omvelt that Ambedkar's conception of original Buddhism does not err on the debit side. Buddhism without *karma-rebirth* framework does not necessarily delegitimatise itself. All the schools of classical Buddhism had arisen owing to the urge to resolve contradictions and inconsistencies. These contradictions were not always mutually compatible, but each one of them could be internally consistent. And still they could be called the different versions of Buddhism. If Sautāntrika, Vaibhāṣika, Yogācāra and Mādhyamika could be accepted as different formulations of Buddhist thought, there should be no reason why Ambedkar's reconstruction is to be profaned. His reconstruction has some advantages over the traditional Buddhism, it explicitly recognises modern values like materialism, secularism and scientific rationality. Ambedkar, through his reconstruction places Buddhism on the frontiers of religion from where one can have a constructive and critical dialogue not only with other religions and other sects of Buddhism but also with non-religious social approaches such as Liberalism, Marxism and Scientism.

# 9

# Checks and Balances in Buddhist Ethics

## I

Buddhist ethics is squarely based upon the following foundational doctrines or presuppositions for moral actions: That all things are inter-dependent, and therefore, have no independent existence. This implies the view that there is no independent, permanent self or ego. Everything is part of an ever-changing flux. The names we give to things are mere conveniences. The chair one sits on, for example, is never the same from moment to moment. Of course, it is impossible to have a different name for how things are at every moment. So names are convenient designations of sets of similar states. The situation is the same with the self. There is no separate permanent self. There is only the flow of mental and bodily experiences. One's name is a convenient designation for all one's *skandhas*, bodily parts, volitions, ideas, etc., taken together. So words are just conventions, practical designations which impose an unreal veneer of permanence on things. The pie of reality can be cut in different ways. We, as human beings, because of our practical needs, cut it up into objects and persons.

This may be necessary, but we must realise that these names do not stand for what is ultimately real. Ultimate reality has been characterised in many ways by Buddhist philosophers throughout history. Some see it as a flow of atoms, others as a flow of ideas, still others, as totally beyond conception.

To come back to persons. If the self has no substantiality then we are all in the same flow as everyone else. Surely we are more similar to our peers than we are to the zygotes we once were. As Śantideva says in the *Bodhicaryāvatāra*, "If I can identify with drops of sperm and blood from which I originated, why can't I identify with the people around me?" If one views one's own interest as equal to those of others then in realising that no one wishes to suffer, one should wish to free all people from suffering. Compassion arises along with a sense of equality and identify with others.

## II

Given the considerations as the above it would be of interest to see in what sense Buddhist morality engages itself to have cessation of suffering as its goal. The Buddha catechized and discoursed with a diverse set of people, with varying motives and intentions, different purposes, ends and views of life. Summarily speaking, the corpus of moral teaching may be distinguished into ordinary ethics and path ethics, designed, as though, for two types of people. Understand that most people are concerned about what they consider their self-interest to be, ordinary ethics sets out to convince people that they will have better lives if they live decently. If you control your anger, people will be less likely to become angry with you. So they will be nice to you and it will be easier for you to be happy. This is ordinary ethics.

Now over to path ethics. On the path of dharma ethical behaviour is exactly that way of acting which will lead one and all beings to enlightenment. Path ethics makes possible the transformation of all experience into something positive. Borrowing an example from the Dalai Lama we can make it clear. An enemy comes to be as a friend because when someone harms us, he or she affords us an opportunity for practicing patience.

## III

In the context of philosophical concerns, one may ask whether following rules (deontological ethics), considering consequences (teleological ethics), or virtue ethics, is a correct ground of moral judgement from the Buddhist point of view. Since Buddhist ethics is a practical path aiming at enlightenment, it might seem one would opt for consequentialism. On the other hand, Buddhists have always believed in the usefulness of following rules. The prohibitions of the eight-fold path regarding moral conduct, not to kill, steal, lie, misuse sex or become intoxicated seem to endorse rule following. Could one then characterise Buddhist ethics as a form of rule utilitarianism? One should follow the rules chosen in relation to the goal of helping all sentient beings to achieve enlightenment, and thereby the cessation of suffering. This is no less true, *pari passu*, that Buddhism holds that rules can be broken out of compassion to avoid very bad consequences. One could lie to save a life. There is even a story of a Bodhisattva who killed a pirate to save five hundred people from shipwreck. But rules may be broken only with great caution. It is too easy to fall into what Kant called "the natural dialectic", (*Critique of Practical Reason*, 108), that is, to set up a smokescreen of apparently ethical reasons to cover up one's motive of self-interest. One can, for example wind-up verbally abusing or even harming someone one dislikes on the pretext of protecting someone who really does not need protection at all or at least not that much. So not only must rules be broken with great caution, but also with wisdom and compassion. Any action, conforming to rules or deviant, has to be in-formed by metaphysical insight. One must not practice stupid compassion, such as shielding a vicious murderer from the authorities. One has to be trained in selflessness through the acquiring of virtuous habits. The development of a strong moral character is the best preparation while dealing with dilemmas in which one must whether or not to follow the rules.

## IV

The virtues traditionally enjoined in Buddhism (generosity, patience, effort, good conduct, concentration and wisdom, in short, the *pāramitās*) are all rooted in the denial of a permanent unchanging self or soul that is capable of existing independently of an interconnected ever-changing universe. Accordingly, selfishness is seen as absurd.

Each of the virtues is bipolar, in having a practical and a *dhārmic* aspect. Patience, seen at the ordinary level of moral life is useful for achieving one's goals. At the path level, patience is viewed as a method of overcoming clinging. At the highest level, it is practiced as a result of the insight that all that exists is a manifestation of enlightenment. Generosity at the ordinary level is practiced to make one's own life and the lives of others more pleasant. On the path level, it is a reflection of the conviction that there is no sharp distinction between oneself and others. On the highest level, it is a reflection of the wisdom and compassion that is the basis of that is.

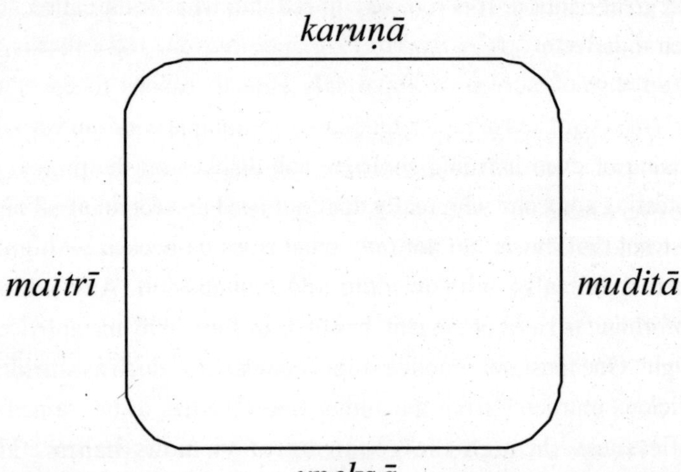

These virtues are not easy to live by, at least in the beginning. The set of four brahmavihāra or immeasurable are designed to make virtuous activity easier. They can be seen as forming a balanced quatrad:

Deeply felt *karuṇā* or compassion can be unbearably painful. Sometimes just reading the newspaper, reading about all the atrocities in the world, can make one want to scream. In Buddhism compassion is balanced by equanimity. This equanimity is a result of the calm and insight achieved in meditation. This allows the moral agent, who is also a meditator, to be completely compassionate without being overwhelmed with despair.

Selflessness leads a Buddhist to want to work unceasingly for others, to fill all his days with acts of loving kindness. This can be exhausting. One is warned not to commit oneself to more than one can handle, so that one will not become bored and tired and give up. One method of avoiding this is to become accustomed to rejoicing in the joy of others. For example, a mother may salve over holiday preparations, shopping for gifts, and cooking. Yet, she is well-rewarded by the joy in the faces of her children and relatives. This unselfish joy is invaluable in preserving motivation. The monks of Ramakrishna Mission or the nuns of Mother Teresa's order are seen to have this joy. They labour unceasingly for others and seem very happy.

The highest source of virtuous behaviour, however, is *bodhicitta* itself. This is the enlightened mind which experiences spontaneously the overwhelming sweetness of welling up of compassion enlivened by wisdom. This produces what Kant calls a holy will. No effort is needed to do good. This enlightened person, a cousin of *sthitaprajña*, a la the *Gītā*, intuits the best thing to be done in every circumstance and does it as unconsciously as breathing, without any motive whatever. How is this possible?

The answer comes from an examination of the deepest ethical questions in Buddhism. In the *Dhammapada* it is said that the enlightened person is beyond good and evil. The discerning "eye" of enlightenment goes beyond distinctions. Then why doesn't a Buddhist dispense with ethics? As long as one does no harm out of excessive attachment and bears no ill-will out of ego-centredness, why not just enjoy *Nirvāṇa* and not lift a finger to help anyone? Why can not one just feel helpful if this is useful to one's own salvation, but not do anything about it? Why can not one just experience the oneness of all being and not act on this at all?

The key is in the experience itself. An analogy can be made between a mother and her only child. The mother will spontaneously help the child. Is this selfish or unselfish? The situation transcends the distinction between selfishness and altruism. The Buddha said to treat all beings as one's only child. It seems that realisation producing the awareness of the interconnectedness of all beings, simultaneously produces the impetus to help them, to see them as being our cherished child.

Let me return to a more detailed consideration of rules, virtues and consequences. Kant introduced what may be called rational absolutism. It was an attempt to make morality both objective and discoverable through the intellectual effort of each person. It could be compared to a mathematical system like Euclidean geometry. If you understand the system, you will arrive at the same answers to geometrical problems as every other person who solves the problem. As in mathematics, the key notion in Kant's ethics was consistency. Kant believed that if a person wants to know what is moral, he or she need only ask what can be acceptable, consistently, for all rational beings. For example, if one wants to know if stealing is acceptable, one needs to decide whether everyone may steal or not. One need merely imagine how one would feel about having others steal from oneself. Clearly it is more rational to will that no one steal. Kant, it is well known, formulated this principle of consistency in the following way. So act, so that the principle or the maxim by which you act can be willed universally.

The major problems with this view are that (a) moral rules can conflict, and (b) carrying out the rules can sometimes have terrible consequences. For example, what if one must lie to save someone's life? Or, what if one must break a promise in order to avoid causing someone's death. Kant's theory does not seem to allow one to do this. The rules are always binding. Further, if the moral agent universalising the rule is not a good person, the rule he or she decides should be followed may be different than the rule a good person will derive.

Act-utilitarianism insists that there is only one moral rule—so act, so that for the greatest number pleasure is maximized and pain is minimised. This is supposed to be close to common sense, but there are difficulties. Suppose, for example, torturing one person to death gave great pleasure to 10,000 people. The happiness of the "audience" of 10,000 might outweigh the unhappiness of the tortured victim. Further, there is no room for justice on Bentham's view. Consequences in terms of pleasure and pain are the only factors to be considered.

Much contemporary ethics attempts to derive a moral theory that preserves the good elements of Kant's and Bentham's views without the difficulties these-views imply. One of these compromises is rule-utilitarianism. This is the view that the point of having moral rules is to benefit human beings because following these rules generally results in increasing happiness or decreasing suffering. This still does not tell us what to do in a particular case when we know that following a rule might cause great suffering. We seem to need a rule to tell us when we may break rules.

## VI

Buddhist ethics represents a compromise between rule-following and concern with consequences in terms of human suffering and happiness, a compromise achieved by means of an ethic of virtue. The ultimate goal of Buddhist ethics is the overcoming of suffering. Yet, human beings cannot always know what will overcome suffering in the long run. We are limited by (a) ignorance of all the circumstances involved in a moral decision, and (b) our own tendencies towards self-deception. For this reason, Buddhist ethics has always recognised the importance of moral rules such as those forbidding killing, theft, lying, and sexual misconduct. These rules are meant to protect us from our own ignorance and protect others from our mistakes in judgement. Therefore, moral rules are to be respected. Even the Buddha loved to describe himself as washed around by rules of virtue or *śīla.*

There are, of course, cases where moral rules needs be broken: cases where considerations of compassion may require that they be broken. We must sometimes lie to prevent dire consequences. In such cases, however, the rules should be broken reluctantly because one cannot be absolutely sure that one has correctly judged the consequences.

Moral rules are to be understood in terms of compassion and not social conventions. Social conventions are to be respected only insofar as it would be uncompassionate to flaunt them. Some cultures, for example, would consider it a case of sexual misconduct for a male doctor to examine a woman. Yet, a doctor should do so anyway to save her life, but discretely. For example, in a fundamentalist religious society in which men are not allowed to look at the bodies of women other than their wives, he should allow his patient to be mostly covered except for the areas that must be examined.

Buddhist virtues are listed in various ways. A common way of such listing is the set of six *pāramitās*, with *prajñā* to crown it all.

A virtuous person is less likely to be self deceptive when breaking rules. Such a person should have the generosity and wisdom not to act for selfish reasons or trivial reasons.

What finally is the complete picture of Buddhist ethics? I would suggest that it functions as a system of checks and balances, similar to a federal government. The rules are there, and these are like the legislature. But the rules should be broken to prevent very bad consequences. This is like the executive branch. And virtues are needed to guide one's judgement of the consequences. This is like the judiciary.

## VII

There is another aspect of Buddhist ethics that needs exploring, the *reciprocity criterion* outlined in the *Sigālovāda Suttanta*. There the Buddha outlines a plan for society indicating that the obligations of some are contingent on others fulfilling theirs. The most significant case involves the reciprocal obligations of husband and wife. The husband should respect her, show courtesy, be faithful, hand over authority to her, and provide her with adornment. When the wife is thus ministered to by her husband, she will love (show love) in the following way: by performing her duties well, by hospitality to the kin of both, by faithfulness, by watching over the goods he brings, and by skill and industry in discharging all her business. The role of the wife expressed here are very significant because people has been following the laws of Manu which stipulate that a woman is first subject to her father, then her husband and should he die, to her son. In the Buddhist view there is no mention of obedience. And even the role ascribed to the wife is contingent on the good offices of the husband. Similar reciprocal roles are outlined for parents and children, teachers and students, among friends, employers and employees. In the Suttanta, the Buddha expresses the duties in the optative mood (should) and predicts the others apostrophe, responses in the indicative. When the Buddha spoke to the wife, he spoke to her in terms of duties and described the good behaviour of her husband as a natural development from her conduct. This is a case of implied reciprocity.

Now how does this system of reciprocal duties fit into the system of checks and balances? There does seem to be a sort of rule-utilitarianism implicit in this text, for the duties outlined are intended to produce a harmonious society.

At first sight justice seems to be absent in the list of Buddhist virtues. Perhaps this is, as Hume suggests, because justice is needed precisely where virtues are lacking. But as the *Sigālovāda Suttanta* explains, reciprocity, which is a kind of justice, is important for a peaceful and happy family and society. In this sense, reciprocity, this is part and parcel of a concept of justice that fits nicely into a Buddhist system of ethics. And so the theory of checks and balances between rules, consequences and virtues comes to a full circle.

## VIII

The Buddhist synthesis of three types of ethical theories, deontology, rule-utilitarianism and virtue ethics can support some aspects of multi-culturalism without supporting such cruel practices as selling children into slavery. It is also an alternative to colonial ethical systems which try to impose a Christian ethic on a non-christian population. Practices in any society must be judged by whether or not they are consistent with virtues such as generosity, and whether they can be practiced compassionately. They must be fair in the sense that they are in accordance with explicit or implicit agreements among the people affected. But the practices considered acceptable may nonetheless vary from society to society. There is room for tolerance towards different cultural traditions while opposing those that violate the spirit of compassion. Of highest importance for Buddhist ethics are compassion and loving kindness which are ultimately the wellspring from which any truly moral conduct must emerge. Without this there may be only heartless and rigid regulations. Surely kindness and compassion are of great saving value for our turbulent age.

# 10

# Closing Thoughts

In keeping with the Buddha's last admonition, *ātma dipo bhava,* be a lamp unto yourself, the preceding chapters, have reviewed Buddhist ethics as the ethics of self–perfection. The basic features of Buddhist ethics, keeping closely to Theravāda accounts, have been deliberated upon. But that does not complete the story of Buddhist moral thinking. There is more to it as reflected in the development of Mahāyāna. In the present context, the book proposes to undertake some discussion about Mahāyāna ethics. Theravāda and Mahāyāna, it may be noted, are not unrelated. Even as Mahāyāna developed new metaphysical thinking in terms of Yogācāra and Mādhyamika, the ethical point of view too developed further, without making a radical departure. The new developments can be noted in the following sequel.

Among the four noble truths, ethics is a key aspect of the fourth, the true paths. Given that we are suffering terribly, taking account of the sources of this suffering and the prospect of its cure, the question arises as to what therapeutic action is indicated. True paths, as prescribed by the Buddha, are detailed as three trainings: training in ethics (*Śīla)*, training in meditation (*Samādhi)* and training in wisdom (*Prajñā*). Within this framework, ethics is taken as a foundational discipline of restraint. It involves the avoidance of non-virtue. When true paths are presented as the Eightfold Path, then ethics refers to the right speech, right action and right livelihood.

At the same time, there are profound dimensions within the trainings in meditation and wisdom as well. For instance, the four sublime attitudes *(brahma-vihāra):* loving-kindness, compassion, sympathetic joy and equanimity are included in the training in meditation. Buddhist meditation *per se* is an ethical activity in so far as it involves systematically cultivating attitudes of care and calm, while displacing contrary unwholesome attitudes. Within the training in wisdom, the second of the Eightfold Path right thought crucially involves turning the mind away from craving and intentions to harm (*rāga* and *dveṣa).* The meditation on virtuous attitudes bears fruit as everyday dispositions, intentions and motivations that are caring and calm rather than acquisitive or malign.

It is said by Śāntideva that just as the body which is constituted with hands and other limbs should be protected as a single entity, the whole world should be treated as undivided one so far as its nature is concerned. If it is taken as divided, it would suffer. One should remove sufferings of others because it is suffering like one's own. A thirsty person is compared to a monkey desiring fruits. It is metaphorised as poison. It is advised to eradicate the root of such thirst through the weapon of wisdom (*Dhammapada* 24/2 and 24/5).

Buddhism has not been without a socially formative dynamism and sense of direction. Such sense of social direction grows directly out of one its basic notions, i.e., the radiation of good will and good moral character. The method of social change is that of the individualised radiation of virtue out into society by persons of moral integrity. Just as social improvement in the sum of the individual self-improvement of the members of society, so society must or may improve by individuals in an individual way. The power of the example of a good man is great and may do more to change the character of a society than all manner of political schemes and policy statements. There is a kind of contagion of good will. The character of a man affects all that he does. There are no impersonal deeds. A non-coercive, non-authoratarian, democratic society is envisaged by Buddhism, where leadership comes only from good moral character, where all goods are held in common possession.

In Mahāyāna ethics, the above elements are fully present, and to them is added the bodhisattva ideal. The bodhisattva is the image of human perfection, and, to an extent, it is comparable to the ideal of *sthitaprajña,* though there are differences. But the two ideals are related.

The rhetoric implicit in the very term Mahāyāna is that this epithet is predicated upon utter dedication to the welfare of the greatest number of living beings, which is to say, all of them. This is to be the prime motivation of ethical living. Rather than seeing compassion as one of several enlightened attitudes (as in Theravāda) to which we may eventually attain, universal compassion is brought forward and celebrated as the core of the path, its vital element in the beginning, middle and end. This is what distinguishes Mahāyāna ethics from Theravāda moral thinking.

The Mahāyāna Buddhist path puts this compassion into practice through six perfections or *pāramitās.* These are compassion-based virtues of generosity *(dāna)*, ethical discipline *(śīla)*, patient forbearance *(kṣānti)*, enthusiastic effort *(vīrya)*, meditative stabilisation *(dhyāna)* and wisdom (*prajñā*). Yet the ethics of the second perfection is not something new in Mahāyāna, it is a mental attitude that turns away from harming other beings. It preeminently includes the ethics of restraint, avoiding non-virtuous actions, but it also includes the ethics of gathering virtues (*puṇya*) such as the six *pāramitās* themselves, and the ethics of acting for the welfare of living beings. Since the practice of the six *pāramitās* is a synopsis of all practice on the Mahāyāna path, one may conclude that the ethics of the second *pāramitā,* taken in the broadest sense, includes all bodhisattva practices. In general, nothing in life is utterly disconnected from ethics; all bodhisattva practices take place within the framework of an ethic of compassion.

What could be the argument for compassion as the prime motive in moral life? Mahāyāna works have the following argument pattern. Happiness is the purpose and meaning of life. All beings want happiness and none want suffering. Real happiness, our fullest flourishing and well-being, is found only through helping others, while unhappiness and needless misery arise from harming. Happiness is interdependent. This position is based on universalising the logic of the Mahāyāna Buddhist teachings, and may be as follows. In accordance with the Buddhist ethics of self-perfection, the highest human ideal is perfect Buddhahood, to become *samyak sambuddha*. This is the purpose of human life, the complete and perfect enlightenment of a Buddha. The happiness of buddhahood is attained by dedicating oneself utterly to the welfare and happiness of living beings, compassionately seeking to free all from misery, and the attainment of Buddhahood for oneself and others. This requires the insight that all things and persons exist only interdependently, lacking any essential nature of their own. This follows from a moral interpretation of the *pratityasamutpāda.* No one is an island, but under the determination of *hetu* and *pratyaya*. Hence the ethical instruction that we should seek harmlessness towards other living beings and beyond that to care for them, help them, just as much as we are able. We should do what we can do to help others now, and we should also strive to improve our capacities so that we can harm less and help more. This other-focus is in fact the only path to our *own* fulfillment. Buddhist ethics is proposed in view of a non-solipsistic world of persons (if not of selves), and being empty of any limiting private ego with any intrinsic nature, we have no way of existing at all, let alone existing happily, apart from our deep connections with others. Our conative and affective life is directed towards others. Emptiness of all things not only allows room for ethical distinctions and moral choices about how best to help and least to harm, it is what makes them possible. This view of ethics is integral.

How does *śunyatā* figure in the context of ethics? How does a bodhisattva develop powerful compassion for beings whose fundamental nature is empty? It is argued that meditation on *śunyatā* can in many ways deepen our compassion and the capacity to help. Since all beings seek happiness and avoids pain, there is at base no difference among beings, myself and others. If that be the case, then it becomes possible to realise that there is no independently existing self over here that ought to be protected and satisfied to the exclusion of or even at the expense of other persons out there. In this manner of viewing it becomes possible to develop a deep sense of closeness and relatedness to others. This is what makes Buddhist altruism possible based upon a metaphysics of *śunyatā.*

It has often been asked how in the absence of an intrinsic self ethics can be possible. Who is the moral agent? Who is it that cultivates loving-kindness? One, in raising such questions forgets Hume who found no argument for the existence of a self in the Cartesian fashion, and still developed a system of ethics. In many ways Buddhism anticipated Humean conclusions with similar or alike premises. It is true that the notion of an ethical agent who is somehow also permanent and intrinsically existent is fundamental in many systems of religious ethics. In our times Derek Parfit has argued forcefully along Buddhist lines of thinking. In point of fact the notion of an intrinsically existing moral agent or self has not borne analytic scrutiny. It is more or less an article of faith or "presupposition" as Kant would have it. Buddhism may and does not have the notion of a self in the sense of *ātman* but it does admit existence of *persons* or *pudgala*. We must remember that once the Pudgalavādins formed a powerful sect of Buddhism. The point is that the anti-foundationalist teaching of Buddhism, namely, that all things are empty of any intrinsic nature (*svabhāva*) is equivalent to saying that all things exist by way of being conditioned by *hetu* and *pratyaya*, i.e., the basic teaching of *pratityasamutpāda*, is by no means unfit for a workable basis for ethics. The Buddhist argument may be put as under: If the soul or intrinsic self of the individual makes moral choices and acts, then is it changed or not changed in the process of acting? If it is not changed, then moral choices seem to have no consequences for me since the real me, my eternal intrinsic self, is never affected by them. But if I am affected by my choices, then I must be something that is constantly changing, something that exists in contingency. In that case, how could I be an eternal or essential self? Hence, the notion of an eternally existing self is no inalienable part of the moral choices and their consequences.

The core of Buddhist ethics is: At least, do not harm, even if you cannot help others. We should seek not to harm other living beings. Ethics is an attitude of abstention that turns one's mind away from harming others. Perfecting one's ethical discipline means utterly abandoning the inclination to harm others. This, of course, does not and cannot be measured by actual success in keeping others free from harm. In spite of the Buddhas who arose in the past, there is unfathomably vast numbers of beings who suffer terribly. Whether the living beings in the external world are actually free from harm or not is not the point here. The practice of ethical discipline is the habituation within your mind to an attitude of abstention that turns away from harming them, we need not be discouraged on account of the fact that due to circumstances beyond our control, the harm suffered by living beings around us has nonetheless increased. We should purify ourselves, our minds of the intention not to harm and doing what we can to minimise harm. The ideal of non-harm is like Polaris, a star by which to steer.

The moral interpretation of *pratityasamutpāda* is crucial for understanding Mahāyāna ethics. The deepest roots of hostility, anger, malice and other harm–related mental afflictions are the delusion that we exist independently. Clinging to the self-existent person that we believe is our true self, we fear its annihilation in death. This leads us to regard other living beings as our enemies, when in fact our true enemies are always the mental afflictions themselves. We tend to anger, for example, as a necessary protector against those who oppose our interests. Śāntideva in the *Bodhicaryāvatāra* makes dire warnings about the consequences of anger.

Harvey Aronson has noted that anger is valued in many countries and traditions as of positive value in struggles for social justice and intrinsic to the healthy emotional life of individuals. Does it mean that anger has a positive value? We should distinguish aggression and aggressive impulses from a more realistic or healthy anger that might arise in reaction to an inappropriate violation. In other words, perhaps a sense of outrage at violations of oneself or other living beings can be morally good or neutral, as long as it is not associated with an intention to harm.

In the last ten years, a growing body of psychological research seems consistent with the Buddhist view that our inclination to harm others is grounded in a deluded and reifying view of our own nature. Terror Management Theory argues that our situation as mammals who foresee our own deaths creates an implicit and persistent anxiety. Each culture provides its members with ways of controlling this anxiety. People can be tolerant of others when their available psychological and cultural resources keep anxiety about death at a manageable level. Expressed attitudes and behaviour towards people perceived as different change in the presence of stimuli that raise implicit anxiety about death. Studies in the psychological sources of terrorism have confirmed the Buddhist view. When we express negative attitudes about Muslims, and vice versa, the anxiety about death rises, and terror acts arise.

We all have the potential to reach happiness. To fulfill that potential we must not only seek to minimise harm but also do what we can, starting where we are now, to help living beings. We should intentionally foster, cultivate and strengthen within ourselves the inclination even the determination, to alleviate their misery and help them towards happiness. Buddhism is a complex web of systems for training the mind in virtue.

Pali Buddhism or Theravāda emphasises the cultivation of *maitrī* (loving-kindness) as a part of self-perfection. What does it really mean? It is said that *maitrī* must be experienced as love for oneself. One must truly wish well for oneself and know oneself as loveable and beloved. How can self-love could be a virtue? Loving *only* oneself does not help others. But a man who does not love himself can never love another. The sphere of love, once first well-established right here, can be gradually expanded to include all living beings. This follows from what the Buddha had said through the analogy of a mother's love for her only child. It is that kind of love that is to be extended to all others.

Studies in Attachment Theory in Psychology have shown that our capacity to care for others cannot proceed from inner deprivation. It has to be founded upon earlier satisfaction in emotional sharing, which creates both an inclination and capacity for fuller and deeper sharing. Our styles of connecting and relating with others are shaped by our early experiences with our own mothers.

Buddhist ethics teaches that we must be able to love ourselves, wish well for ourselves, and then gradually learn to see others as similar cases of beings who, like ourselves, want happiness and do not want suffering. This gives us a chance to become persons, and a core teaching. Bringing to bear the insights of Attachment Theory, it also suggests that we are able to begin systematically cultivating the vast love of a bodhisattva only by working from a wide and secure base, the deep conviction that we are loveable and have long been love through innumerable births.

The core claim of Buddhist ethics, that happiness arises from dispositions or mental states designated as virtue, would seem to be amenable to empirical investigation. One branch of contemporary psychology, known as Positive Psychology, has made findings that support some traditional Buddhist teachings. But scientific investigations apart, it remains a fact that right now, as the Buddha said, a man *is* wounded by an arrow. Thousands of children are starving. Our planet is toxic with the detritus of our ravenous consumption. In the face of death, the way to find meaning and purpose is to serve the welfare of others. The Buddhist says: Like all who seek happiness, you should set firmly in mind, and keep as your compass, a determination to help other beings. There lies the promise of self-perfection.

To bring the discussion to a close I would like to present some tentative suggestions on how the concept of *anātma* or selflessness, a core doctrine of Buddhism, can be used to form the basis of a Buddhist theory of social justice, without endangering Buddhism's primary focus on individual salvation. The concept of *anātma* could be employed to link the apparently conflicting goals of social justice and individual enlightenment.

In the Buddhist idiom the process of spiritual growth is linked to the healing of existential sickness. Life is suffering, but it can be cured through therapy, if proper remedy is applied. *Duhkha* or suffering stems from our subconscious desires, or thirst, as variantly called in order to indicate its blind and vehement driving force. Again, the blind nature of desire causes the root sickness of human suffering, and hence it equated with ignorance, *avidyā*. All other diseases are merely symptoms of this foundational ignorance. The main symptom is the attachment to the objects of the senses, and to something inside oneself, the one so-called self.

The Buddha had suggested the availability of a remedy, based on the diagnosis. Enlightenment or happiness (*sukha*) is opposed to suffering, and it is inherent in the individual. It means is that happiness may be achieved by curing the root sickness within ourselves.

The Buddhist emphasis on self-healing, the individual's search for enlightenment could have been the reason why Buddhism did not development a social philosophy in the contemporary sense. And it is a non-solipsistic world-view as far as moral matters are concerned. The Buddha did not intend to create a political ideology, yet he did not ignore the existence of the other. The classic statement of the Buddha's moral non-solipsism occurs in the Vinaya text: "Walk, monks, on tour for the blessing of many people, for the happiness for many people out of compassion for the world, for the welfare, the blessing, the happiness of *devas* and human beings" (*The Book of the Discipline,* Vol. IV, 28, tr. I. B. Horner). Interpretations of this passage have varied. Early Buddhists understood this passage to mean that the Buddha asked his disciples to work for others. But it was also taken to mean that in order to help others one must first become enlightened and therefore healed. This point made in the dictum that one who is sick cannot cure others. And hence the followers of the Way occupied themselves with the work of self-healing, and became relatively passive in the domain of society. We must not, of course, profane the Mahāyāna project of postponing one's enlightenment and engage in social benevolence. The idea finds scintillating expression in Śāntideva's *Bodhicaryāvatāra*:

For as long as space endures

And for as long as living beings remain,

Until then may I too abide

To dispel the misery of the world

(X.55. tr. Stephen Batchelor, LTWA, Dharamsala, 1979).

In the light of such passages as the *Metta sutta* or the celebrated concept and ideal of brahmavihāra, which is somewhat foundationally important for a Buddhist's lifestyle, it can hardly ever be said Buddhism takes no head of the interpersonal dimension of human experience. To say that would be a gross over simplification. Now coming to the therapeutic pattern of Buddhist teachings, it remains to add that the original idea that one who is sick cannot cure others came to be radically transformed by the bodhisattva ideal in Mahāyāna phase of the doctrine, adumbrated in a new set of scriptures in Sanskrit. There appeared a new socio-religious atmosphere embodied in the figure of the bodhisattva.

The importance of the bodhisattva ideal for our purposes is that the bodhisattva cures himself by curing others. The *Vajradhvaja Sūtra* has the relevant passage: "A bodhisattva resolves: I take upon myself the burden of all suffering, I am resolved to do so. I will endure it and...All costs I must bear the burdens of all being, and the whole of living being I must rescue, from the terrors of birth, of old age, of sickness, of death and rebirth". (trans. Conze et. al, 1964, 131).

The bodhisattva's resolve is not simply compassion towards others. For the bodhisattva, the essence of *anātma* is that there is, in fact, no difference between himself and others. *Anātma* is not merely the denial of a cogito-like Cartesean self or a substantial soul as in Christianity, it also implies a non-dualistic view of me and others, and asserts the extension of one's own existence beyond the boundary of the private ego or the self to encompass that of others. Others, for the bodhisattva, are nothing more than the extension of his own existence. He embraces all others as we, which includes not just me and *you*, but also *them.*

The concept of *anātma* thus opens the avenue to social awareness and the necessity of engagement. Vimalakirti is a typal Mahāyāna bodhisattva figure, who identifies the sickness of all living beings with his own, stating, "I am sick because all sentient beings are sick; when the sickness of all sentient beings have been cured, mine also will be cured". (5446). For this reason he postpones his own enlightenment and chooses to be born again and again until everyone else attains salvation. The spiritual value of this choice lies in its active involvement in society and in the notion that society is an extension of one's own existence. Vimalakirti instructs bodhisattvas to convert the experience of sickness into something positive, something that generates wholesome, striving energy. Because of his sickness, as commentary goes to explain, he should take pity on all others who are sick. He should know of the suffering of countless aeons of past lives, and because of this he should think of the welfare of all beings. Instead of generating grief and vexation, a bodhisattva should constantly give rise to striving energy. Here we see that the experience of suffering becomes transformed into the potentiality of curing others. Without the experience of sickness one cannot cure another. The experience of illness becomes a catalyst. Instead of causing the bodhisattva is to seek release from his own pains by entering into the bliss of *nirvāna*. Illness for him should be a great leveller, reminding him of the essential brotherhood of man inherent in the shared suffering of existential sickness. Conscious of his link to all beings, the bodhisattva should increase his resolve to come to their aid and succour. To look back to the *Vajradhvaja Sūtra* once more: the Bodhisattva resolves, "To the limit of my endurance I will experience in all states of woe, found in any world system, all the abodes of suffering, and I am resolved to abide in each single state of woe for numberless aeons, and so I will help all beings to freedom, in all states of woe that may be found" (Conze et. al trans. 1964, 131).

Why does the bodhisattva choose to adopt the suffering of others? How does this enable him to help them and thus to lead them, and ultimately himself as well, to enlightenment? It is because only by fully embracing the experience of others, their sickness and suffering entailed, can he fully realise himself as identical to them. The experience of absorbing himself into their sickness, and of thus realising his essential identification with them, is the only means by which the bodhisattva may develop wisdom and compassion, the qualities that he needs in order to show others the cause of their sickness. Similarly, he may use these same qualities of wisdom and compassion in order to discover why he himself also suffers.

The exposition above is anchored on the level of soteriology, and not social philosophy. The bodhisattva seeks to cure himself of suffering by gaining enlightenment, but because of his profound understanding of the doctrine of *anātma*, he realises that to so he must first help cure all other sentient beings. This entails an active engagement with their suffering, and furthermore, a willingness to find personal inspiration in the struggle against suffering in general.

# A Glossary of Terms in the Text

Ānanda (Sanskrit): A cousin and favourite disciple and personal attendant of Sākyamuni Buddha. As a personal attendant for many years, he is said to recite the sutras from memory at the First Council (held at Rajagraha) after the death of Sākyamuni.

*Anātta* (Pali), *Anātma* (Sanskrit): The term usually meant "no-soul", "no-self", "non-ego", "a denial of permanent soul". According to the Buddhist teaching there is no permanent soul that trans-migrates after death to another body. Buddhism anātman is the ideal condition Extinction.

*Bodhisatta* (Pali), *Bodhisattva* (Sanskrit): Bodhi means enlightenment and Sattva means being. The etymological meaning of the term is "Enlightenment Being". The term denotes that one who seeks enlightenment as a Buddha and before Buddhahood he should do all possible altruism deeds and dedicates to the salvation of others. The bodhisattva is the Mahāyāna ideal of a perfected individual, who postpones by choice his own individual liberation for the sake of ameliorating the sorrows of other beings.

*Bodhicaryāvatāra*: A classical text comprising Mahāyāna ethics written by Śāntideva. This text is arranged in ten chapters and begins with the importance of the cultivation of the thought of enlightenment. It includes the six traditional perfections (*pāramitās*), substituting "mindfulness" for the tradition "giving" (*dāna*) and "awareness" for the traditional "morality" (*śīla*). It also offers two meditations- the equality of self and others and others for self.

*Brahmavihāra*: Blessed meditational states, namely *maitrī, karuṇā*, *muditā* and *upekṣā*.

*Dhamma* (Pali), *Dharma* (Sanskrit): It comes from the root *dhr* means to hold, to bear, truth, norm. In Buddhist teachings dhamma is known as *Ārya* satya (the Four Noble Truths) concerning the facts of existence.

*Dhammapada* (Pali), *Dharmapada* (Sanskrit): "The Path of Religion", "Stanzas (pada) on the Teaching". This is also an early text in the Pali Buddhist canon (the second book in the *Khuddaka Nikāya* of the *Sutta Pitaka*).

*Dukkha* (Pali), *Duhkha* (Sanskrit): Sorrow or suffering. The unavoidable-Anxiety produces from the touchability with the mundane pleasures. The first of the Four Noble Truth ("*sarvaṁ duhkhaṁ*") propounding the Dharma is realised by the Buddha in his awakening.

*Enlightenment:* According to the Hinayāna tradition, enlightenment means the cessation of ignorance and of conflicting motion, and therefore freedom from the compulsive rebirth in *saṁsāra*. But the Mahāyāna tradition believes that enlightenment requires not only cessation of ignorance but also compassion and skilful means to work with the bewilderment of all sentient being.

*Nibbana* (Pali), *Nirvāṇa* (Sanskrit): The term denotes the blowing out of a flame, the extinction of the flame of desire that occasions countless rebirths within *saṁsāra*. According to the Hinayāna tradition, it means extinction of avidya, but the Mahāyāna tradition defines it as "attainment of truth" or enlightenment.

*Pañcaśīla* (Sanskrit): The purpose of the five precepts (*Pañcaśīla*) is to help the suffering millions to break out of this chain of rebirth, infirmity and death by right living through adherence to the following:

(i) refrain from injuring living beings, (ii) refrain from taking that which is not given, (iii) refrain from all forms of *kāma*, sexual desire, (iv) refrain from all falsehood, in word and deed, and (v) refrain from worldly enjoyments no drugs, no drinks, no sloth.

*Pāramitā* (Sanskrit): The term denotes the ultimate ideal of spiritual perfection and it is an important conception of Mahāyāna tradition. It refers to those virtues which guide and assist the aspirants on the path of perfection and also represents the life of bodhisattva, the signs of enlightenment. The six *pāramitās* are *dāna*, *śīla*, *kṣhanti* virya, *dhyāna* and wisdom or *prajñā*. Sometimes the list includes *upāya*, *pranidhāna*, bala and *jñāna*.

*Sangha* (Sanskrit and Pali): "Group"; "order"; the community of Buddhist monks; one of the three refuges, the other two beings, the Buddha and Dhamma. In a Mahāyāna sense, the *mahāsangha* of greater sangha also includes the lay community. The third of the three refuges was founded by the Buddha continued to the present day in Theravāda Buddhism.

*Tanhā* (Pali), *Trishnā* (Sanskrit): 'Thirst'; 'craving'; the word denotes inordinate desire. This is one of the *nidān* of the bhavacakra, which is the cause of duhkha and needs to be eliminated.

*Theravāda* (Pali): "The Doctrine of the Elder"; "teaching of the elders"; the orthodox sect of Buddhism derived from the earliest texts which have been preserved in the Southeast Asia, namely, Burma, Sri Lanka, Thailand, Laos and Cambodia.

# Bibliography


Ahir, D.C. (2004), *Buddhism and Ambedkar,* B.R. Pub. Delhi.

Ambedkar, B.R. (1959), *Buddhism is Ethics,* Poona University, Poona.

————(1957), *The Buddha and his Dhamma*, People's Education Society, Bombay.

Banerjee, B. and Chaudhuri, S. (ed.) (2005), *Buddha and Buddhism,* The Asiatic Society, Kolkata.

Banerjee, N.V. (2000), *The Dhammapada*, M.M. Pub. Ltd, 2000.

Bapat, P.V. (ed.) (1986), *2500 Years of Buddhism*, India. Ministry of Information and Broadcasting, Publications Dept., Delhi.

Barua Dipak Kumar (2003), *An Analytical Study of Four Nikayas,* Munshiram Manoharlal, New Delhi.

Bhandarkar, D.R. (2000), *Aśoka,* AES, New Delhi.

Bhattacharya, Vidhushekhara (2007), *The Basic Conception of Buddhism,* Universal Voice, Delhi.

*Bodhicaryāvatāra (Śantideva)* K. Crosty and A. Skilton (trans.) (1995), *Śantideva: Bodhicaryāvatāra*, Oxford: Oxford University Press; Paramananda Sharma (trans.) (2001), *Śantideva's Bodhicaryāvatāra*, Aditya Prakashan, Delhi; Stephen Batchelor (trans.) (1979), *Śantideva's Bodhicaryāvatāra*, X55, LTWA, Dharamsala.

Chandra Ramesh and Mitra Sangh (2003), *Buddha: A Revolutionary and Reformer,* Commonwealth, New Delhi.

Chitkara, M.G. (2007), Encyclopaedia of Buddhism:A World Faith, Vol. XXI, A.P.H. Publishing Corporation, New Delhi.

*Complete Works of Swami Vivekananda*, 9th ed. (1964), Calcutta.

Conze, E. (1951), *Buddhism: Its Essence and Development*, Cassirer, Oxford. (2nd paperback edition, 1974).

——— (1954), *Buddhist Texts Through The Ages*, Bruno Cassirer, Oxford.

———(1962), *Buddhist Thought in India*, George Allen Unwin, London.

———(1967), *Thirty Years of Buddhist Studies*, Bruno Cassirer, Oxford.

Dalai Lama, The (1999), *Ethics for the New Millennium,* New York.

———(1977), *The Four Noble Truths*, Harper Collins Publishers, India.

———(1995), *The Path to Enlightenment*, Snow Lion Publications, Inc. Ithaca, New York, U.S.A.

———(2012), *Beyond Religion*, Harper Vollins, New Delhi.

*Dhammapada Pali and Suttanipata: Pali Text with English translation* (2004), F. Max Muller and Fausboll,V, re-edited by O.P. Pathak, Bharatiya Vidya Prakashan, Delhi.

Dharmasiri, G. (1989), *Fundamentals of Buddhist Ethics,* Golden Leaves Publishing, Antioch.

*Dialogues of the Buddha (1956-1957), Sacred Books of the East, trans.*Rhys Davids, London, Luzac, Vols. I, II and III.

Dravid, N.S. (1995), Udayanacarya-*Atmatattvaviveka*: *Translation, Explanation and Analytical-Critical Survey*, IIAS, Shimla.

Dutta, N. (1970), Buddhist Sects in India, Firma K.L. Mukhopadhyay, Calcutta.

———— (1978), *Mahāyāna Buddhism*, Motilal Banarsidass, Delhi.

Eliade, M. (ed.) (1987), *Encyclopedia of Religion,* Macmillan, New York.

Epstein, Mark (2007), *Psychotherapy without the Self*, New Haven, Yale.

Fu, Wei-hsun Charles and Wawrytko, Sandra A. (ed.) (1991), *Buddhist Ethics and Modern Society*, Greenwood Press, London.

Gellner N. David (2001), *The Anthropology of Buddhism and Hinduism:Weberian Themes,* Oxford University Press, Delhi.

Gethin R.M.L. (2007), *The Buddhist Path of Awakening.* One world Oxford.

Harvey Peter (1990), *An Introduction to Buddhism: Teachings, History and Practices,* Cambridge University Press.

————(2000) Buddhist Ethics: Foundations, Values and Issues, Cambridge University Press.

Horner, I.B. and Coomaraswamy, A.K. (1948), *The Living Thoughts of Gotama Buddha*, Cassel, London.

*Journal of Buddhist Ethics - 3* : 1-13, October, 1999.

Keown, D. (ed.) (2000), *Contemporary Buddhist Ethics,* Surrey, Curzon.

Keown, D. (2003), *Oxford Dictionary of Buddhism,* OUP.

——————(1992), *The Nature of Buddhist Ethics*, Basingstoke: Macmillan.

Lamotte, E. (1976), The Teachings of Vimalakirti, (Lamotte's 1962 French Translation of the Vimalakirti-nirdeśa, rendered in English by S. Boin), Pali Text Society, London.

Lindtner. Chr. (1982), *Nāgārjuniana: Studies in the Writings and Philosophy of Nāgārjuna*, Cophenhagen: Akademick Forlag.

Lopez, Donald, S. (ed.) (2008), *Awakening the Mind, Lightening the Heart* by *His Holiness the Dalai Lama,* Library of Tibetan Works and Archives, Dharmasala.

Mahalasekera and Jayatilleke, *Buddhism and Society.* UNESCO, Paris.

*Majjhima Nikāya*, 3 Vols. (1958), edited by P.B. Bapat and R. Sankrityayana Pali Publication Board, Nalanda.

Matics Marion, L. (2007), *The Bodhicaryavatara of Śāntideva: Entering the Path of Enlightenment,* Motilal Banarsidass, Delhi.

Mūlamadhyamakakārikā (Nāgārjuna) (1986), trans. by David Kalupahana, Albany: State University of New York Press.

Mungeswar B. and Rathore A.S. (ed.) *Buddhism and the Contemporary World: An Ambedkarian Perspective,* Bookwell, New Delhi.

Nāgārjuna (2007), *Bodhicitta – vivaraṇa*, CUTS, Saranath.

Narain, A.K. and Ahir, D.C. (1994), *Dr. Ambedkar, Buddhism and Social Change*, B.R. Publishing Corporation, Delhi.

Nattier Jan (trans.) (2007), *The Bodhisattva Path: Based on the Ugrapariprccha, A Mahayana Sutra,* Motilal Banarsidass, Delhi.

Niebuhr, Reinhold (1963), *Moral Man and Immoral Society: A Study in Ethics and Politics*, SCM Press Ltd., London.

Nithiyanandam. V. (ed.) (2002), *Buddha's Doctrine of Suffering and Salvation,* Global Vision Pub., Delhi.

Nyanatiloka, M. (1956), *Buddhist Dictionary,* Colombo: Frewin and Co.

Oldenberg Hermann (2006), *Buddha: His Life, His Doctrine, His Order,* Pilgrims, Varanasi.

Omvedt Gail (2003), *Buddhism in India: Challenging Brahmanism and Caste,* Sage Publication, New Delhi.

Pande, G.C. (1957), *Studies in The Origins of Buddhism*, University of Allahabad.

Panikkar, K.M. (1947), *Survey of Indian History*, National Information and Publication, Bombay.

Pathak. Om Prakash and Gaur Veena (ed.) (2000), *Abhidhammapitaka Puggalapannattipali* (with English Translation), Eastern Book, Linkers, Delhi.

Prebish Charles, S. (ed.) (1995), *Buddhism:A Modern Perspective,* Satguru, Delhi.

Rachels, J. (1993), *The Elements of Moral Philosophy,* New York, McGraw Hill.

Radhakrishnan, S. (1969), *The Dhammapada with Commentry*, Oxford University Press.

Romila Thapar (1968), *Interpretations of Ancient Indian History*, Wesbyan University, Connecticut, U.S.A.

Reich, W.T. (ed.) (1995), *Encyclopedia of Ethics,* New York, Macmillan.

Rhys Davids. T.W. (1900), (trans. from Pali), *Buddhist Sutta*, Oxford Clarendon Press.

——————(2000), *Buddhism: Its History and Literature*, Asian Educational Services, New Delhi.

Roy, P. (2011), *Mapping The Bodhicaryāvatāra,* Indian Institute of Advanced Study, Shimla.

Saint – Hilaire J. Barthelemy (2000), *The Buddha and His Religion,* Asian Educational Services, New Delhi.

Samyutta Nikāya (1942), trans. by Caroline A.F. Rhys Davids, 6 Vols. Pali Text Society, London.

Sangharakshita (2006), *Ambedkar and Buddhism,* Motilal Banarsidass, Delhi.

Śāntideva, *Bodhicaryāvatāra* (2001), trans. by P. Sharma, Aditya Prakashan, New Delhi.

Sangharakshita, B.A. (1959), *Survey of Buddhism,* Indian Institute of World Culture, Bangalore.

Sen, Amulyachandra, *Aśoka's Edicts,* Calcutta, Indian Publicity Series. n, d.

Singh, Amar (2007), *Buddha's Original Logical: The Sautrantika Analytical Philosophy,* Eastern Book Linkers, Delhi.

Spiro, Melford E. (1971), *Buddhism and Society-A Great Tradition and its Burmese Vicissitudes*, George Allen and Unwin Ltd., London.

Stcherbatsky, Th. and Obermiller, E. (ed.) (2006), Abhisamayalankara – *Prajñāpāramita – Upadeśa – Śāstra: The Works of Bodhisattva Maitreya,* Sri Satguru, Delhi.

Tachibana, S. (1926), *Ethics of Buddhism*, London, Curgon.

*The Sutta-Nipāta*, (trans.) from Pali (1973) by V. Fausboll, *The Sacred Books of the East*, Vol. X. Motilal Banarasidass, Delhi.

Thich Nhat Hauh (1998), *The Sun My Heart*, Full Circle, New Delhi.

Vaidya, P.L. (1960), *Ac tasāhasrikā Prajńā-pāramitā Sūtram* (text), Mithila Institute, Dharbhanga.

Vidyasagar I.S. (2005), *Concept of Humanism of Dr. Ambedkar,* ABD Publishers.

Vijaṛa, Sister, *The Sutta Nipata*, Sarnath, Mahabodhi Society. n, d.

Vivekananda, Swami (1957), *Selections from Swami Vivekananda*, Advaita Ashram, Calcutta.

Wallin, D.J. (2007), *Attachment in Psychotherapy*, New York.

Wang, Touxuan (2001), *Buddhism and Deconstruction*, Curzon Press, Surrey.

Wardwer, A.K. (1977), *Indian Buddhism*, Motilal Banarasidass, Delhi.

Warnock, Mary (1961), *Ethics Since 1900*, Home University Library, London.

Warren, H.C. (1953), *Buddhism in Translations,* Cambridge, Harvard University Press.

Wayman, Alex (1977), *Unitying The Knots in Buddhism*, Motilal Banarsidass, Delhi.

Williams, P. (1989), *Mahāyāna Buddhism*, Routledge, London.

———(2000), *Buddhist Thought*, Routledge, London and New York.

W.K. Frankena (1973), *Ethics*, Prentice-Hall, New Jersy, 1973.

# Index